Women Under Attack

Victories, Backlash, and the Fight for Reproductive Freedom

by the Committee for Abortion Rights and Against Sterilization Abuse

edited by Susan E. Davis

South End Press pamphlet no. 7

DEDICATION

We dedicate this pamphlet to our friends and sisters, Sarah Eisenstein (1946-1978) and Joan Kelly (1928-1982), who showed that "bread and roses" means a commitment to fight for human needs, in all their richness and diversity.

Sarah taught us that thinking through the hardest political questions must be the basis for our organizing and struggle. Although she did not live to see the completion of the first edition of this pamphlet, it was Sarah who initially urged that writing a pamphlet which clarified our thoughts and ideals on reproductive issues and their wider political significance was an important task, and who helped determine its shape and direction. Her sense of collectivity and political and intellectual clarity inform whatever is best and most enduring in what we have written.

Joan, a leading feminist theorist, activist, historian, and teacher, was deeply committed to the struggle for reproductive freedom and social justice. She touched the lives of all who knew her. She taught us about struggle, about dignity, and about the human capacity for endurance. Joan's clarity of vision, sense of purpose, profound capacity for love and life, and the ease with which she bridged the seemingly disparate worlds of academia and political activism are an inspiration to us all.

In the future, in all the work we do together, Sarah's and Joan's courage and social vision will remain our touchstones and move us forward.

First edition. Typesetting, layout, and production by Sebastian Möll and South End Press. Cover design by Cynthia Peters and Loie Hayes
South End Press, 116 St. Botolph St., Boston, MA 02115
Manufactured in the USA.

Library of Congress Cataloging-in-Publication Data:
Women under attack. (South End Press pamphlet; no.7)
Bibliography: p.
1. Pro-choice-movement—United States. 2. Birth Control—United States. 3.Women's Rights—United States. I. Davis, Susan E. (Susan Elizabeth). II. Committee for Abortion Rights and Against Sterilization Abuse (New York, NY).
HQ767.5. U5W66 1988   363.9'6   88-26350
ISBN 0-89608-356-X

Table of Contents

Acknowledgments

Revising this pamphlet was a far more ambitious task than any of us in the CARASA editorial collective ever imagined. Recognition for the many long and dedicated hours required to edit this work go to Sue Davis, Phyllis Gelman, Kristin Booth Glen, Harriet Lazarowitz, Susan Ritz, Karen Stamm, and Anne Teicher.

Those responsible for primary research and writing of particular chapters include:

Eleanor Bader, freelance journalist, columnist for the *Guardian Newsweekly,* News Editor of *New Directions for Women* magazine, and activist in the New York Pro-Choice Coalition, for Chapter 7.

Sue Davis, freelance writer/editor, Book Editor for *New Directions for Women,* representative of All-Peoples Congress in the New York Pro-Choice Coalition, and author of a novel on reproductive freedom, for the Introduction, Chapters 1, 6, and 9.

Kristin Booth Glen, long-time activist in the many movements for social change, New York State Supreme Court Judge, and adjunct professor at New York University and New York Law School, for Chapter 5.

Margaret Phillips, graduate of Barnard College with a degree in anthropology, currently directing a job training program for women on public assistance in Bushwick, Brooklyn, for researching Chapter 8.

Nancy Romer, Associate Professor of Psychology and Women's Studies at Brooklyn College and an activist in the feminist movement, for Chapter 2.

Special thanks are also due to Dr. Vicki Alexander, Peter Aschenbrenner, Dr. Wendy Chavkin, Janet Gallagher, Christina Greene, Sarah Gruhin, Dr. Stanley K. Henshaw, Frances Borden Hubbard, Joel Krieger, Rosalind Petchesky, Dr. Helen Rodriguez-Trias, Barbara Zeluck, and Steel Bellman & Levine.

Todd Jailer, Cynthia Peters, and Loie Hayes at South End Press, who at different stages were most helpful and devoted to this project, made our task much easier.

In the years since the 1973 Supreme Court decision swept aside laws prohibiting abortion, the question of whether abortion should be legal, safe, and accessible remains a major political issue. It is a litmus test for political candidates at all levels of government. It is both denounced and defended from the pulpit. It is a matter of life and death for those who work in or use women's health centers which are targets of harassment or terrorist attack. It is a modern Holy War.

Why is abortion, which can be one of the most private decisions a woman will ever make during her lifetime, so prominently in the political spotlight? Why, as feminists and progressive people, do we see abortion as a leading edge of political struggle?

The Committee for Abortion Rights and Against Sterilization Abuse (CARASA) was founded in New York City in 1977. That year saw a turning point: Congress passed the Hyde Amendment prohibiting Medicaid funding for abortions. In the face of this setback, CARASA published *Women Under Attack: Abortion, Sterilization Abuse, and Reproductive Freedom* in 1979 to assert a feminist analysis of abortion in the context of the broader definition of reproductive freedom. The pamphlet was widely distributed and used by women in all walks of life, including students, activists, and health care workers. This pamphlet is a completely revised edition of that groundbreaking work.

While this new work retains the same political rigor and thoughtful analysis, our vision of reproductive freedom has broadened since 1979. It has become less defensive through the experience and practice of 15 years. We understand that women's efforts to control their reproductive capacity have always been, and continue to be, a process of struggle. Many gains remain since the legalization of abor-

Workers World Photo

1

Peg Averill/Liberation News Service

tion, but there have also been losses. Our increasing understanding propels us to struggle around new issues of reproductive freedom: the new reproductive technologies and the possibilities of abortion and sterilization abuse related to AIDS.

We have come to appreciate the particular ways individual women are affected by the lack of choice in their lives, depending on their class, race, sexual preference, physical condition, marital status, and age. Recognizing these differences and incorporating them into our analysis, we reaffirm that the only way to defend our victories and win reproductive freedom for *all* women is to speak up, fight back, educate, and organize. It is to support this continuing struggle for reproductive freedom that this pamphlet has been revised.

Chapter 1

What Is Reproductive Freedom?

Since the resurgence of feminist consciousness in the 1960s, women have fought and won many political battles, including the right to legal abortion. Once women's place was considered to be in the home and only a small percentage worked outside it. Today women are nearly half the workforce, making inroads in all professions, job categories, political offices, and skilled trades from which they had been systematically excluded.

Discrimination based on gender is being challenged daily by scholarly research, scientific study, and sheer grit and determination as women demand all the privileges and benefits a society can offer. Bastions of institutionalized sexism—from women's lower wages to who gets up when the baby cries at 3 a.m.—are being questioned, challenged, and changed.

In order for women to participate fully and freely in society, an essential condition must be met: Each woman must be able to control her own life. A woman must be free to decide for herself, with or without a partner, when and how she will or will not have children. Women of all classes, races, and ages, regardless of disability or sexual identity, must be guaranteed the full range of social, economic, and political conditions and choices so that every woman can make and act on informed decisions about her sexuality, her reproductive capacity, and every other aspect of her life.

The term "reproductive freedom" encompasses women's many demands and needs. Yet because women are not a homogeneous group, we have been subjected to vastly varied forms of oppression. For example, women as a group are seen as inherently more suited to childrearing because of their childbearing capability. But poor, young, or mentally ill women and lesbians regularly lose custody of their children, and women with disabilities are routinely discouraged from becoming pregnant. Because disproportionately large numbers of people of color are poor and are blamed for their poverty, large percentages of Native American, Puerto Rican, and Black women have been the victims of state population control policies, resulting in racist, genocidal sterilization abuse.

The struggle for reproductive freedom requires a thorough analysis of the many forms of women's oppression. It invariably points to a radical transformation of society. Essential to this transformation is the elimination of sexist, racist, ageist, homophobic, and economic oppression, as well as of the oppression of people with disabling conditions. Though that process promises to be long and arduous, the vision offered by reproductive freedom is both profound and moving.

From Reproductive Rights to Reproductive Freedom

The decision to become pregnant or to abort is private, but it must also be made within a social context. The general notion of rights in U.S. society is based on the idea of "freedom from"—freedom from government power that interferes with our activities and particularly our private decisions. Rights do not generally refer to the power or access necessary to *act* on those decisions. The "right" to legal abortion means only that the government can no longer interfere with a woman's choice by penalizing or imprisoning those who have or perform abortions (see Chapter 5). This is obviously a critical first condition, but the choice to abort—or to have a child—is also based on a whole series of social and ecnonomic variables, such as the availability of reliable, safe contraception; access to prenatal care or funded, safe, legal, accessible abortion; jobs; medical care; and social services like childcare, education, and housing. The ability to make a real, free choice about childbearing requires not only legal rights, but also affirmative access to the necessities that allow us to control our lives. This is why the issue has moved beyond reproductive rights to reproductive freedom.

The prerequisites for reproductive freedom can be broken down into a number of categories, some of which are sure to change and shift as conditions change in the years ahead:

1. *Legal, safe, accessible abortion for all women regardless of age, race, class, or economic status.* Having the legal right to abortion is meaningless if a woman cannot afford one or if there are no convenient facilities where abortions are performed in a safe, supportive environ-

Reproductive freedom demonstration, Cherry Hill, N.J., 1982.

ment. Women must be free to make decisions about abortion without spousal veto, parental restraints, or any kind of judicial procedure.

2. *Freedom from sterilization abuse.* No woman or man should be coerced into being sterilized because of lack of available alternatives, economic or social conditions, race, religious or ethnic background, or confinement in a prison, medical, or mental institution. The decision to become sterilized must be the result of informed consent based on complete and understandable information.

3. *Sexuality and lesbian rights.* Women must be free to express their sexuality in diverse ways, without coercion by either men or the state. They must be able to choose whom to love, including the right to live openly and without fear as lesbians. Until that is guaranteed, all women can be victims of homophobia. Lesbians must have access to alternate forms of insemination and conception, and adoption, so they can become mothers if they wish. Lesbians who are already mothers must have their custody rights recognized and respected.

4. *Access to safe, effective, low-cost contraceptives and comprehensive, quality sex education.* All people, no matter what age, religion, sexual orientation, disabling condition, or marital or economic status, must be well informed about sex and must be able to obtain safe, reliable contraceptive devices. Developing new, safer, more effective means of birth control for both men and women is a top priority. This requires user control over research, development, and distribution of

contraceptives. Everyone should be fully and accurately informed about AIDS and other sexually transmitted diseases so s/he can act responsibly.

5. *Childcare and medical care.* Childcare must be recognized as a public, collective responsibility, with a comprehensive, nationwide, yet community-controlled system of free, 24-hour, quality childcare. A comprehensive system of quality, user-controlled medical care for all is equally necessary.

6. *Safe jobs at livable wages and affordable housing.* In order for women to be able to live with dignity, true bodily integrity, and absolute freedom from either physical coercion by or economic dependence on men, they must be guaranteed safe jobs with adequate wages equal to those men earn and livable, affordable housing. Sexual harassment on the job, and violence in our homes and on the streets, must be vigorously prosecuted.

7. *Reproductive technologies.* All safe means of promoting fertility must be available to everyone regardless of race, sexual orientation, disabling condition, or economic or marital status. Technology should be used for women's benefit, with women's needs the primary concern. Women must not be used as guinea pigs.

8. *Freedom from stereotyped gender roles.* Society defines women in terms of their reproductive capacity: All women are viewed as mothers, potential mothers, former mothers, or nonmothers. Warnings that women without children will feel unfulfilled or be lonely in later years and implications of selfishness make women feel obligated to have children or feel guilty if they do not. Women must be free from these oppressive stereotypes in order to freely choose whether to have children. Those who choose to have children should be freed from mother stereotypes so they can work outside the home if they so wish. Parenting responsibilities should not be based on gender.

Attaining these prerequisites cannot automatically guarantee reproductive freedom but will go far toward that goal.

Chapter 2

Contested Terrain: The Historical Struggle for Fertility Control

For centuries women have used an enormous variety of fertility control methods, attesting to the importance of such control to women. Yet reproduction has also been an ideological battleground on which men, women, and the state have struggled for control over women. Determining who has such control is one measure of the reigning ideology of any culture.

Early Fertility Control

As far back as 1850 B.C.E.,* Egyptian women used vaginal pessaries (suppositories killing or blocking sperm), as did Indian, African, and Middle Eastern women. Vaginal douches of many kinds have been used around the world: Aristotle recommended the use of oil of cedar or olive oil; women of Sumatra used tannic acid. The Old Testament refers to vaginal sponges. Djuka tribes of (Dutch) Guyana used condoms to catch semen inside the vagina, and instructions for manufacturing condoms for men appear in North American home remedy books in the 19th century. Among Australians of the Parapitshuri Sea region, ovaries were surgically removed from girls chosen to be collective prostitutes for the men of the tribe.

The "rhythm method" and natural decreased fertility brought on by extended breast-feeding were used by Inuit and other Native American, Ancient Egyptian, and modern European women. Numerous home remedy abortifacients, either taken orally or inserted into the uterus, included those suggested by Greek physicians in the time of

*Before the Common Era

Nero and those detailed by German folk medicine. Inserting instruments into the uterus and scraping fetal tissue are documented among sources as varied as 10th-century Persian physicians and 20th-century Greenland Inuit tribes. Attempts to self-induce abortion—by jumping from heights, lifting heavy weights, taking hot baths, etc.—were also common. According to a survey of anthropological literature, 125 out of 200 tribes studied reported use of abortion.

To limit population and maintain desired sex ratios, some cultures have also practiced infanticide. Aristotle and Plato suggested it for eugenic purposes. An ancient Roman law entitled the father to decide whether to keep a child, attesting to men's power over reproduction. Infanticide has also been documented among Australian and Native American peoples, Polynesians, and specifically for female newborns among Chinese, Indians, North Africans, and Tahitians.

More Recent U.S. History

Until the mid-19th century, the U.S. government had no systematic legal postion on birth control or abortion. The Catholic Church did not prohibit abortion before "quickening"—fetal movement beginning around the fourth month of gestation—until 1869.

The Industrial Revolution produced great changes. People moved from the countryside, where more children meant more agricultural production, into urban areas, where children cost more than they produced. Enormous hardships on the job, overcrowding and lack of resources at home, cruel practices of child labor, as well as the rigors of endless childbearing on women's health influenced many women, including Black women slaves, to try to limit the size of their families. The ideology of the period stressed planning and investment of resources. Concomitantly, women sought to invest their limited energy and resources in smaller numbers of children. Use of abortion and often unreliable birth control was widespread among women of all social classes.

By the 1870s three diverse forces joined together to outlaw abortion and establish male control over women's fertility. Growing ranks of licensed physicians sought to monopolize women's health care by eliminating women's access to birth control and abortion and by outlawing midwives, the primary reproductive health care providers until that point. Eager for more workers to be (re)produced, industrialists favored this result. Support also came from eugenicists who wanted greater procreation by middle-class women of northern European descent and less among immigrants from southern and eastern Europe.

The Family Limitation Movement

The progressive political movements in the first quarter of the 20th century were complex and dynamic. The suffragist movement, whose leadership was primarily white and middle-class, was deeply conflicted about broader social issues, including fertility control. The working-class movement for unionization and socialism was equally conflicted about feminism and fertility control, as well as generally exclusionary and sexist toward women. Nonetheless, it was in the context of working-class organizations that the first wave of the modern fertility control movement began.

Social activists Emma Goldman and Margaret Sanger held mass street meetings in New York City. Sanger wrote a popular column for women in the Socialist Party daily newspaper, *The Call*. Many members of the left-wing International Workers of the World and the Socialist Party printed and distributed Sanger's famous "Family Limitation" leaflet, instructing tens of thousands of women in birth control techniques. These organizers articulated the idea that reproductive self-control was critical to equality between the sexes and to improving women's position in society.

This movement was set back by two factors. The first was the aggressive prosecution of family limitation movement activists, especially Margaret Sanger, through the Comstock Law, which prohibited "obscene" material (including birth control information) from being distributed by mail. Long jail sentences imposed severe strains on the leadership and limited organizing. Yet these women might have braved the storm more heroically had they had more support from the suffrage and working-class movements.

Just when persecutions of family limitation movement leaders began in earnest, the socialist movement came under sharp attack from the government and the workers' movement split on the question of political direction. The left wing, which supported the family limitation movement, wanted to continue a trade union, mass movement approach to social change. The right wing favored an electoral approach and backed away from too much confrontation with the government it sought to join. It opposed the family limitation movement, viewing it as a threat to the working-class family and an "unimportant," nonpolitical issue.

By the 1920s, Margaret Sanger and her more moderate feminist colleagues sought the protection of the medically-based, industrialist-funded population control movement, dominated by eugenicists. They sought to impose fertility control (though not abortion) on U.S. women,

APRIL 20, 1920
MY MOTHER DIED
OF AN
ILLEGAL ABORTION

Rachel Johnson/Guardianphoto

particularly those poor and Black for whom they thought it was "socially appropriate" to limit fertility. This same group subsequently sought to use modern contraceptive techniques to control population growth in colonial regions of Asia, Africa, and especially Latin America. U.S. investors and government leaders were increasingly worried by the desires of Third World peoples for freedom and self-determination. They theorized that liberation movements could be undermined by coercing Third World women into using birth control. Testing new contraceptive technologies on women without their consent became a common practice. Many women did receive the contraceptives and sterilization they needed, but often at great cost to their health and political freedom.

For family limitation activists, half a dream was better than none. They supported organizations like Sanger's American Birth Control League, the forerunner of Planned Parenthood, which lobbied for government endorsement and funding. By the 1960s, the birth control movement was controlled by the government, technocrats, doctors, and international capitalists.

European Parallels

At the same time that U.S. women struggled for access to fertility control, European women demanded the same rights. For example, after the Russian Revolution of 1917, a national governmental women's bureau led by Alexandra Kollontai fought for women's rights as family members, and political activists. It demanded the legalization of abortion and distribution of contraceptives, as well as a host of other social changes offering women more freedom, such as collective kitchens, childcare, and an end to the sexual double standard. Abortion was legalized in 1920 as a temporary health care measure, but was repealed in 1935 in a general attack on progressive social laws and policies. In Germany, the women's movement, allied with the progressive workers' movement, lacked an independent feminist approach and was soundly defeated by Nazi population policy-makers, who outlawed abortion and instituted eugenics and genocide as a central platform of social control.

Political theater at pre-*Roe v. Wade* abortion speak-out, New York City.

The Second Wave

In the years preceding 1968, the lives of North American women shifted significantly. Living standards improved and white women began to join the paid workforce in larger numbers. The development of the highly reliable birth control pill allowed young women to become more sexually active. The emphasis on birth control for Third World and poor North American women by the now-established population control organizations had an ironic double effect: While racist in intent and effect, it was also liberating to have birth control publicly accepted and available. Abortion remained a necessity although its illegality kept it expensive and dangerous.

Many women who participated in the civil rights and anti-war movements in the 1960s questioned their position in society, particularly traditional expectations about sexuality and reproduction. Women began to articulate the need to control their reproductive capacity if they were to be liberated. They rediscovered feminist theorists who linked reproductive and sexual freedom to the quality of women's lives and to their political, economic, and social power.

Distribution of gynecological information, contraceptives, and illegal abortion referrals became increasingly politicized. Women rallied to expose the cruel reality of women's abortion experiences: Abortion rarely involved anesthesia or sanitary conditions and was usually a humiliating and life-threatening experience. Estimates range from 200,000 to one million illegal abortions performed annually. Many deaths were the direct result of botched abortions, primarily among poor women, a significant portion of whom were women of color.

By 1968 abortion was a major issue in the emerging women's movement, including demands for reform or repeal of laws limiting abortion. Moderate and liberal feminists sought support from the legal and medical establishments to reform abortion laws. Radical and socialist feminists aimed at repeal of all abortion laws and eradication of the legal and medical establishment's control over abortion. Their goal was "free abortion on demand" so that *all* women, regardless of income, could control their reproductive capacity. Driven by the slogan "the personal is the political," they organized mass mobilizations and independent women's organizations. Their politics included issues of sexual preference, anti-racism, anti-militarism, and working-class involvement in a call for women's liberation. Despite political differences, all feminists united to make abortion a central national issue.

The social and economic climate had also changed. When male workers were in demand in the 1900s, an anti-birth control and anti-abortion policy prevailed. Now lower-paid women workers were needed for service jobs and the burgeoning computer revolution. Many doctors were also outraged by the medical complications and deaths associated with illegal abortion. Others were eager to control yet another aspect of women's health care and garner the profits from legalized, medically controlled abortion. Public opinion was also changing; by 1969, over 60 percent of the U.S. populations in every religious group endorsed abortion as a private issue to be decided by individual women.

By 1970, Colorado, Hawaii, and New York had reformed abortion laws. Hundreds of women poured into New York from all over the country seeking safe, legal, inexpensive abortions. Skirmishes on the legislative and judicial fronts were waged everywhere. Finally, in 1973 the U.S. Supreme Court decided in *Roe v. Wade* that the right to choose an abortion belonged to a woman and her doctor, at least during the first 3 months of pregnancy. This judicial solution would soon open new arenas for struggle (see Chapter 5).

The Movement for Reproductive Freedom

After the *Roe v. Wade* decision, many women discarded their picket signs, believing the struggle was over, even though women in different parts of the country did not have ready access to abortions. Later that year, the issue of sterilization abuse received attention when it was reported that federal funds had been used to sterilize 2 Black teenagers

without their knowledge or consent. In response to this and other abuses, a multinational group of activists formed the Committee to End Sterilization Abuse (CESA) in New York City. Their research revealed the racist population control policy begun in the 1940s that led to the sterilization of over a third of all women of childbearing age in Puerto Rico. A highly successful campaign of propaganda and withholding of other fertility control had been conducted by a coalition of government, big business, and medical forces. Additional studies documented that disproportionately high numbers of Black and Native American women in the United States were also being sterilized.

In response to the Hyde Amendment, radical and socialist feminists in New York City formed the Committee for Abortion Rights and Against Sterilization Abuse (CARASA). Abortion rights and freedom from sterilization abuse were seen as two sides of the same coin, since poor women, denied funding for abortion, might be coerced into sterilization, which, by contrast, was funded 90 percent by the government. Countering racist population control policies was intended to build unity across race and class lines, which had been one of the failings of the family limitation movement. Lesbian activists soon urged the movement to broaden its agenda to include a redefinition of family and to analyze reproduction as it affects the social, economic, and political needs of other groups of women. This process led to the comprehensive, radical demand for reproductive freedom.

With the formation of the Reproductive Rights National Network (R2N2) in 1981, an organization with 80 member-groups, the movement pursued an increasingly complex range of issues. Although R2N2 disbanded in November 1984, in part because of differences in strategies for combatting racism and homophobia (see Chapter 8), its successes and failures provide lessons for theory and practice in the future.

Chapter 3

Contraception, Abortion, and Sterilization Today: What Choices Do Women Really Have?

The goal of reproductive freedom is to ensure that women and men are able to make reproductive decisions without social, economic, or political coercion. For vast numbers of women and men there are multiple factors, both hidden and overt, which narrow or even dictate if and how people make decisions. These need to be identified so we can act on them and create alternate empowering institutions, policies, and attitudes.

Some factors are personal and involve such internal, subjective frames of reference as a woman's ethnic background or religion; her knowledge of, control over, and feelings about her body; and her partner's willingness or unwillingness to share responsibility. A woman's choice of fertility control also involves such external, objective factors as literacy, income, insurance coverage (third-party payment), availability of information and alternatives, provider bias, risks to health or side effects, ease of use, and perceived effectiveness.

Although contraception, abortion, and sterilization are all means of controlling fertility, they are radically different in their technology and in their impact on individuals and groups of women. Despite the apparent neutrality of technology, control over it determines to whom it is provided, by whom, and for what purpose. Research and development of methods and surgical techniques have been directed by the predominantly white male medical profession and profit-motivated pharmaceutical companies and are devoted almost exclusively to controlling female fertility while ignoring the male role in conception.

15

Chemical or surgical intervention is favored over noninvasive, woman-controlled methods, and risks due to contraception are described by manufacturers as minimal. Pharmaceutical corporations, striving to maximize profits, do not respond to the needs of individual women, but collaborate with the bureaucratic national and international population control organizations to determine what contraceptives will be produced.

The range of choices available to women, already limited by the various internal and external factors of individual women's lives and by the lack of control over technology, also varies by race, nationality, age, disabling condition, and class. These differences will be discussed in Chapter 8. What is important in assessing various methods of fertility control is whether a particular method contributes to or takes away from an individual's choice and control.

Methods of Contraception

The following discussion of different contraceptive methods briefly analyzes their advantages and disadvantages. No method is 100 percent adequate or effective. Consistency and proper use are critical to

**COMPARISON OF CONTRACEPTIVE METHOD
TYPICAL AND LOWEST REPORTED FAILURE RATES, UNITED STATES.**

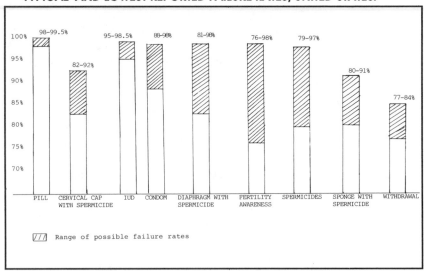

Source: <u>Contraceptive Technology</u>, 13th and 14th Revised Editions.
Irvington Publishers, Inc., New York, New York, 10003. 1986, 1988. Table 9.1.

maximizing effectiveness. Charts summarize the percentages of women using which methods, according to marital status and race, as well as rates of effectiveness. Recommended for a more comprehensive discussion of all types of fertility control is *The New Our Bodies, Ourselves* (see Suggested Readings).

Oral Contraceptives

When first marketed in the United States in 1960, "the pill" dramatically altered the world of fertility control and sexual behavior. It contains estrogen, progestin, or a combination of the two hormones, preventing ovulation and therefore conception. It is the most effective nonsurgical contraceptive (98-99.5 percent) and is easy to use, readily available, relatively inexpensive, eagerly dispensed by most health practitioners, and does not interfere with sexual activity. It also offers some protection against pelvic inflammatory disease (PID), protects against ovarian and endometrial cancer, and minimizes menstrual cramps and heavy periods.

But the pill has serious side effects, including increased risk of blood clots, liver tumors strokes, and heart attacks. Cigarette smoking, pre-existing heart disease, diabetes, hypertension, and advancing age

PERCENT DISTRIBUTION OF WOMEN 15-44 YEARS OF AGE BY CONTRACEPTIVE METHOD, RACE AND LATIN ORIGIN, UNITED STATES, 1982.

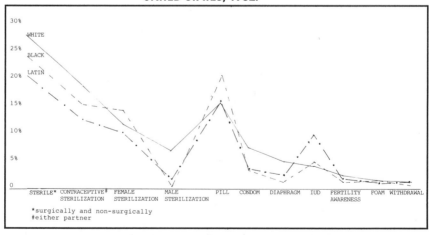

Source: National Center for Health Statisitcs, W.D. Mosher and C.A. Bachrach: Contraceptive Use, 1982. Vital and Health Statistics. Series 23, No. 12. D.H.H.S. Pub. No. (PHS) 86-1988. Public Health Service. Washington, U.S. Government Printing Office, Sept., 1986. Table 8, page 32.

(35 or older) all increase the risks of cardiovascular disease. Cervical cancer has been found in some studies to be significantly increased in women taking the pill, and there is greater risk of fibrocystic breast condition. There may also be a long delay in resuming ovulation and a normal menstrual cycle after use has been discontinued.

Less serious but annoying complications include acne, visual disturbances, breast tenderness, spotting or heavier breakthrough bleeding, and nausea. Depression, changes in sexual desire, and weight gain have also been reported. Therefore, the pill is best used for limited periods by young, nonsmoking, healthy women who are highly motivated not to get pregnant.

Barrier Methods

Five methods physically prevent sperm from meeting an egg. Since they must be used shortly before vaginal intercourse, they require planning, motivation, and a partner's cooperation. Although each has specific side effects, they are safer than the pill or the IUD (discussed later). With the possible exception of spermicides, they do not harm the woman or the fetus should pregnancy accidently occur. Several offer some protection against sexually transmitted diseases (STDs), including AIDS. All but the condom maximize women's control.

• The Diaphragm

The diaphragm, a circular piece of latex or rubber stretched over a spring, is covered with spermicidal jelly and inserted by the woman or her partner through the vagina over the cervix. It must be left in place for 6 to 8 hours after intercourse. Other practical problems include complaints of dripping, messiness, and timing its insertion. Side effects may include recurrent cystitis (bladder infection), allergic reaction, and a foul-smelling discharge or vaginal ulceration. Toxic shock syndrome (TSS) has been associated with diaphragm use in rare cases.

The diaphragm must be prescribed by health care professionals. Racist and elitist assumptions among health care providers—that poor, less educated women, and women of color will not properly use a diaphragm—lead them to write a prescription for pills rather than take the time to demonstrate the diaphragm's use.

• The Cervical Cap

Like the diaphragm, the cervical cap is made of rubber and is inserted by the woman or her partner into the vagina, fitting snugly over the cervix. It has several advantages over the diaphragm. It is less messy, since less spermicide is required; the cap size rarely changes (unlike the diaphragm size that can vary with weight gain/loss and pregnancy); it can safely be left in place for up to 2 days; and some women find it more comfortable. Its primary disadvatage is a limitation on the existing cap sizes and the result that not all women can be properly fitted. Others are unable to insert it. Cervical irritation or erosion is possible, the cap may become dislodged during intercourse, and it may acquire an odor over time.

Until May 1988, it was only possible to obtain a cap in the United States from a practioner conducting a Food and Drug Administration (FDA) study. It has now been licensed, but remains expensive.

• *The Contraceptive Sponge*

Introduced in 1983 and available over the counter, the contraceptive sponge is made of polyurethene and contains the spermicidal agent

PERCENT OF WOMEN 15-44 YEARS OF AGE USING CONTRACEPTION BY RACE, MARITAL STATUS, AND METHOD OF CONTRACEPTION, UNITED STATES, 1982

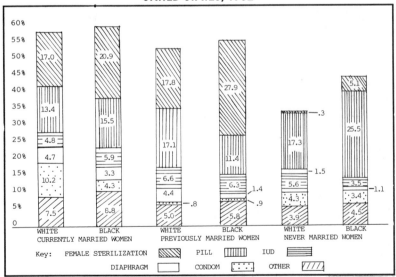

Source: National Center for Health Statistics, W.D. Mosher and C.A. Bachrach: Contraceptive Use, 1982. Vital and Health Statistics. Series 23, No. 12. D.H.H.S. Pub. No. (PHS) 86-1988. Public Health Service. Washington, U.S. Government Printing Office, Sept. 1986. Table D, page 13; Tables 8-15, pages 32-40.

nonoxynol-9. A loop is attached for removal. It must be moistened, inserted into the vagina and over the cervix, and left in place for 6 to 8 hours after intercourse. Its side effects include allergic reaction to and irritation from the spermicide. Toxic shock has been associated with over-long use. Some 6 percent of users require medical assistance to remove it. It is less effective than the diaphragm.

- ### *The Condom*

Condoms are sheaths of rubber or processed collagen rolled onto an erect penis by either partner immediately before vaginal intercourse. (The condom can also be used during anal intercourse for disease prevention.) Besides vasectomy and withdrawal, condoms are the only method of fertility control used by men. Bought over the counter or in vending machines, they come in many styles, colors, and textures, may be lubricated, and may contain spermicidal agents. Ideally, they should be used with spermicidal foams. This combination equals the pill's effectiveness, without major side effects.

The condom has no biological side effects and has a relatively low failure rate (between 88 and 98 percent). Some people complain that condoms diminish pleasure or sensation during intercourse, but many such complaints stem from cultural conditioning or notions of the primacy of male sexual experience.

The condom's greatest, most consistent benefit is that it protects both men and women from sexually transmitted diseases. It is the only "safe sex" method of fertility control recommended to avoid transmission of the AIDS virus. Its use is strongly encouraged in all new sexual relationships or with partners whose risk factors are unknown or questionable, *regardless* of other contraceptive measures.

- ### *Spermicides*

When used alone, spermicidal foams, creams, jellies, or suppositories are the least effective barrier method. Their major advantage is some protection against sexually transmitted diseases. Some people are allergic to particular brands, and some find they make oral sex unpleasant.

Fertility Awareness Methods

Often known as "natural family planning," fertility awareness methods require that a woman observe changes in her body indicating ovulation and then abstain from vaginal intercourse for a number of days. These methods include: (1) the calendar or rhythm method, in which a woman plots the most likely time of ovulation by statistical average; (2) the basal temperature method, where a woman takes her temperature each morning and observes a small rise on the day she ovulates; (3) the mucous or Billings method, where a woman observes an increase in vaginal mucous of a greasy or slippery consistency; and (4) the sympto-thermal method, which combines all three.

Although there are no side effects, the major problem with these methods, resulting in a fairly high failure rate, is that a woman's menstrual cycle can vary widely from month to month, that there is no certainty of how long sperm or ova are viable, and that male co-operation in refraining from intercourse is required. When used with barrier methods, effectiveness is greatly increased. Nevertheless, these methods are the only "acceptable" means of fertility control for some religious women.

Coitus Interruptus

Otherwise known as "withdrawal," coitus interruptus requires that a man pull out of his partner's vagina before ejaculation. However, there is a substantial risk that the preejaculatory fluid contains enough sperm to impregnate a woman. Worrying about self-control and "timing" can often diminish a couple's sexual pleasure.

The IUD

The intrauterine device (IUD), or "loop," is a small piece of variously shaped plastic or copper attached to a string, which is inserted in the uterus by a health provider and which can remain in place for years. Besides a fairly low failure rate, its major advantage is that it requires little of the woman once it is inserted. Because of the small degree of user involvement, the IUD was heavily promoted by health care professionals for poor women in this country and by population control organizations operating in the Third World.

However, the history of the IUD provides a highly controversial case study of the gross failure of a modern method of fertility control. Thrust into the marketplace in the 1970s after inadequate testing primarily in Puerto Rico, the IUD soon created massive health complications, including death and infertility. Another very serious side effect is pelvic inflammatory disease (PID), which can lead to sterility or increased chance of life-threatening ectopic (tubal) pregnancy.

The IUD can also become displaced, perforate the cervix or the uterus, or become embedded in the uterus. If the device remains in place or becomes partially expelled without the woman's knowledge and she becomes pregnant, it is often life threatening. This frequently results in spontaneous abortion, almost always accompanied by infection. Less serious side effects include spotting, heavy bleeding or hemorrhaging during a menstrual period, anemia, cramping, chronic pain, "losing" the string, and difficult removal.

The Dalkon Shield proved to be especially dangerous, causing very high rates of PID, pregnancy, septic abortion, and sterility. Although there was substantial evidence of dangers, including 17 deaths by 1975, its manufacturer, A.H. Robins, never warned users of the risks and did not recall the Shield until forced to in the early 1980s.

Over 2.2 million women in the United States used the Shield; it is estimated that 100,000 women still do so. A 1978 law suit brought against Robins by nearly 200,000 women is still in the courts. To counter the suit, the otherwise profitable company has declared bankruptcy and set aside a fund of $2.4 billion. The plaintiffs sought $7 billion.

Because of the legal cases against Robins, most drug companies lost their IUD insurance and ceased its domestic distribution, finding IUD profits only in sales to international population control agencies. A new IUD—ParaGard Model T 380A—was released in 1988 and costs $140, making it inaccessible to millions of women. It is thought that its copper content may reduce risk of infection. Its use is restricted to women who have had at least one child, who have no history of PID, and who are involved in a long-term, mutually monogamous relationship, which puts them at low risk of contracting a sexually transmitted disease.

Experimental Contraception

A number of methods that rely on manipulating a woman's hormonal system are still in research, are not approved in the United States, or are not widely used. They include:

1. *Norplant subdermal implants* are chemical capsules inserted under the skin in a woman's arm that prevent pregnancy for 5 years. Possible side effects include irregular bleeding and increased chance of later ectopic pregnancy. The method may be FDA-approved in 1988.

2. *Depo-Provera* or DMPA, known as "the shot," is an injection of progestin that prevents pregnancy for up to 6 months. Although not approved for contraceptive use in the United States after intense pressure from women's health activists because of links to cancer in animals, it is used in 80 countries.

Donna Evans/Impact Visuals

Many international feminists oppose this method because of uncertain safety and because, as an injectable, it does not allow for speedy reversal.

3. *Hormone-elaborating vaginal rings,* slightly smaller than a diaphragm, are placed in the vagina for 21 days each month where they release progestins that prevent pregnancy. The rings must be removed during vaginal intercourse and then replaced. They have not been approved for use in the United States.

4. *The mini-pill,* containing only progestin, is theoretically safer than oral contraceptives with estrogen, which is responsible for cardiovascular side effects. Available in parts of the United States since 1973, the mini-pill has still not been thoroughly studied and tested.

5. *Progesterone-antagonist RU 486,* an abortion-inducing drug, is the most controversial and potentially the most significant in terms of women's control over fertility. If taken on the 25th day of the menstrual cycle, it prevents the action of progesterone in the uterus; this induces bleeding within 72 hours. RU 486 becomes more efficient when taken with prostaglandins, virtually eliminating severe bleeding and incomplete abortion, but the combination may create severe cramping.

The availability of RU 486 would radically change the abortion picture since women could abort at home without surgical intervention. Because RU 486 requires only a prescription, abortions would be safer, cheaper, and more private. Some abortion clinics might be put out of business, thus eliminating convenient targets for harassment by the anti-abortion movement. Thus far the "Right to Life" movement has kept U.S. pharmaceutical manufacturers from seeking FDA approval by threatening to boycott company products.

Abortion

When used as a backup for the diaphragm and/or the condom, abortion as a means of fertility control is *safer* than the pill. First-trimester abortions (6 to 12 weeks) performed under legal and medically safe conditions have a much lower risk of death than tonsillectomy or sterilization procedures and *significantly lower risk of death than pregnancy, labor, and delivery.*

Modern methods of vacuum aspiration make abortion a simple procedure. After local or general anesthesia, the cervical opening to the uterus is dilated and a tube attached to a motorized pump is inserted. Suction is used for about 5 minutes to draw out the uterine tissue. Weakness, fatigue, cramps, or nausea may follow, so a short period of rest is recommended. Aftercare instructions are given to prevent infection. Complications such as fever, cramping, vomiting, fainting, or excessive bleeding should be immediately reported to the abortion provider.

Early abortion is also less likely than pregnancy and childbirth to result in or aggravate such serious health complications as phlebitis, varicose veins, anemia, malnutrition, and depression. In fact, these conditions may be reasons why women seek abortions.

Second-trimester abortions involve greater risk. Two procedures are used. Dilatation and evacuation (D and E) may be used from 12 to 20 weeks. In this procedure fetal tissue is removed with instruments, and the uterus is cleaned by vacuum aspiration and scraped with a metal loop. The other procedure is used from 16 to 24 weeks. The abortion is induced by an injection of either saline (salt) or prostaglandin F_2a, which cause contractions and expulsion of the fetus. The D and E is safer, less expensive, and physically and emotionally easier than a saline or prostaglandin abortion.

When abortion is illegal, restricted, or combined with sterilization procedures, high rates of maternal death or serious health complications result. Restrictions on abortion may lead to delays until after the twelfth week (the end of the first trimester) when the risks increase drastically. Before 1973 women were forced to resort to costly, illegal "back-alley" abortions, which were often botched, leading to infections, hemorrhaging, or death; or they tried to self-induce abortions with household chemicals, coat hangers, or knitting needles.

Over 90 percent of U.S. abortions are performed in the first trimester when risks are lowest. In 1983 the risk for all methods of abortion was 0.7 deaths per 100,000 for all women in each age, racial, and geographical group. However, since Black women tend to have abor-

tions later than white women, they face greater risk of abortion mortality.

Statistics show that women who are young and poor are most likely to use abortion. Yet, the right of these women to choose contraception or abortion is the most limited due to parental notification laws (see Chapter 5), adolescent abstinence programs, and the Hyde Amendment.

Several years ago the *New York Times* reported the story of a poor woman "who was on birth control pills but gave them up because of high blood pressure. When she went to a clinic to be fitted for an IUD, she was told that their schedule was full. When her contraceptive foam ran out, she did not have the five dollars for a new supply. That is when she became pregnant." Like many women who get abortions, this woman was not "irresponsible." She was overwhelmed by medical, social, and economic obstacles that often make abortion necessary (see Chapters 6 and 8 for a discussion of these issues).

Most people expect or want to determine the number, spacing, and timing of their children, so abortion plays an integral, essential role in fertility control. There are many reasons why a woman chooses to have an abortion. Frequently, women make the decision out of a sense of responsibility to others—their parents, existing children, and the people with whom they live and work. Some women choose abortion because their fertility control failed, they learned they were carrying a fetus with a devastating genetic disease, they became pregnant as a result of rape or incest, they could not cope with pregnancy, or they changed their mind about being a mother. Whatever the reason, abortion must be available to any woman who chooses not to be pregnant.

Choosing to have an abortion should always be a woman's decision. For some it is complicated and agonizing; for others, easy and clear-cut. For many women, abortion is an emotionally charged experience. Grief or depression may follow an abortion. Yet afterwards most women feel relieved or empowered.

No matter how her decision is arrived at, no woman should be forced to explain her reasons or be second-guessed by family or medical, religious, governmental, or other institutions. Women's right to abortion must be free from the value judgments and pressures imposed by those who oppose legal abortion (see Chapter 7 for a discussion of the anti-abortion backlash) or who have historically regulated women's fertility for their own purposes. The "right to choose" an abortion includes not only the legal right, but access to funds and safe facilities that make that decision realizable. It is an indispensable part of every woman's freedom to express her sexuality, control her body, determine her life, and decide whether, when, and under what conditions to have a child.

Sterilization

Sterilization, the most prevalent form of fertility control in the United States for women over 25, differs dramatically from abortion and contraception. It permanently renders a woman or man infertile.

For women, sterilization is a major surgical procedure done with general or local anesthesia in which the Fallopian tubes are cut, burned, clipped, or otherwise shut, preventing eggs from reaching the uterus. The tubes are reached though an incision in the abdomen or less often through the vagina. Two of the most common methods are laparoscopy and laparotomy. (In the past, hysterectomy was sometimes used for sterilization purposes.) Women can be sterilized at any time, except during pregnancy.

Vasectomy is the male sterilization procedure. Two small incisions are made in the scrotum to cut the vas deferens, the tubes that carry sperm. Vasectomy is a minor operation, requiring only a local anesthetic.

Like all major surgical procedures, female sterilization entails risks of infection, blood clots, and complications due to anesthesia, with rare instances of death. For reasons that are not well understood, a woman's menstrual period may increase in flow and be more painful after sterilization. Regret rates higher than 30 percent have been reported. Regret or depression is generally attributed to poor counseling about the permanence and side effects of sterilization. Women may also feel regret when they have little choice due to such factors as coercion from their husbands or medical difficulties. In less than 2 percent of sterilizations, the procedure may fail or reverse itself. Vasectomy is much safer than female sterilization, but it too can result in infection, failure, and regret.

Since the 1970s sterilization has been promoted by the medical and family planning establishments as an easy solution to people's desire for effective fertility control. Dissatisfaction with the dangers and inadequacies of the pill, IUD, and other methods of fertility control has led increasing numbers of women to accept sterilization.

Sterilization differs historically from abortion and other birth control methods. While abortion has at times been restricted, sterilization has been aggressively promoted among certain groups of women and men deemed "surplus" or "undesirable," including the poor, Native American, Latin, Black, and the mentally incompetent. By contrast, a middle-class woman wishing a sterilization used to be subject to the doctors' rule of "120": that is, the number of her children times her age had to equal at least 120.

Since the early 1900s, state statutes permitted eugenic sterilizations on those considered "feeble minded" or "genetically defective" and are still used in some states to sterilize the institutionalized. Between 1907 and 1964, 64,000 people were sterilized under these laws.

In the 1970s, lawsuits exposed a broad pattern of involuntary sterilization of poor women by government-funded clinics and private doctors. One notorious case involved the involuntary sterilization with federal funds of 12- and 14-year-old Black sisters in Alabama without their parents' knowledge or consent.

Documented abuse has primarily involved poor women of color. Women were sterilized without consent, or consent was obtained on the basis of false or misleading information—commonly that the operation was reversible or that it was free of problems and side effects. Information was given in languages women did not understand; women were threatened with loss of welfare or medical benefits if they did not consent; consent was solicited during labor; and abortion was conditioned upon consent to sterilization.

Abuse may occur in less overt but coercive ways: Social and economic conditions can exert so much pressure that a woman feels she has no other option. Sterilization is promoted with little information about other alternatives. Medicaid and private insurance companies pay for the procedure, but not for contraception.

Statistics suggest that women bear the brunt of these pressures. Among low-income Blacks and Latins, more women than men are sterilized. Those men who choose vasectomies are most likely to be middle-class and married.

Female sterilization in the United States increased 350 percent between 1970 and 1975, and between 1976 and 1982, the rates nearly doubled. The dramatic rise in sterilizations coincided with the virtual elimination of federal funding for abortion and other restrictions on access. The federal government assumes 90 percent of the cost of most sterilizations under Medicaid at the same time that it pays for only a minuscule number of abortions. This funding disparity amounts to a government policy of population control targeted at poor people and people of color. There are no statistics about the extent to which women who rely on Medicaid-funded abortion have turned to sterilization, but the increase in sterilizations and the cutbacks in abortion funding and accessibility appear related. In the absence of adequate income, birth control, childcare, and health care, we cannot assume that the rise in sterilization is a result of "free choice."

Overt and covert forms of pressure have been exploited by population control groups that encouraged sterilization, especially among particular populations of women. All of these factors led to disturbing demographic trends. Black and Latin women, particularly those on public assistance, were more likely to be sterilized than white women using private medical services. Compared with the general population of married women, Black and Latin married women were sterilized in significantly greater proportions. As of 1968, 35.3 percent of all women of childbearing age were sterilized in Puerto Rico, where abortion was unavailable to all but wealthy North Americans. One study showed 25 percent of Native American women were also sterilized. Between 1976 and 1982, the percentage of all currently married women relying on sterilization increased markedly, but the increase was larger for Blacks than for whites.

Sterilization among people of color in this country has had its counterpart in the Third World. Using federal funds, population control advocates exported sterilization programs in the belief that social unrest could be "cured" by diminishing the number of dissatisfied people. This theory erroneously points to overpopulation as the cause of social problems instead of the structure of the social systems in which people live.

Beginning in 1973, women of color, feminists, and health care workers in the United States recognized and responded to the various forms of domestic sterilization abuse. They proposed and lobbied for guidelines to regulate sterilizations in New York City and, in 1977, regulations were passed by the City Council. In 1979 the federal Department of Health, Education, and Welfare (now the Department of Health and Human Services) adopted regulations patterned after the New York City law.

The federal regulations condition payment to the provider on the provider's compliance. They include informed consent in the woman's or man's own language, a 30-day waiting period between consent and the operation, and information that the operation is considered both permanent and irreversible and about alternatives. Consent may not be obtained during abortion or childbirth. Hysterectomies for sterilization purposes are not funded, nor are sterilizations for people under 21, in prison, or those legally declared incompetent.

Despite lack of adequate enforcement of the federal and New York City regulations, they represent a major victory in the movement to achieve reproductive freedom. They provide a strong warning to potential abusers. Groups that traditionally supported abortion rights, such as Planned Parenthood, Zero Population Growth, and the Assocation for Voluntary Sterilization (now the Association for Surgical Contraception), adamantly opposed the regulations on the grounds that they deprived women of "freedom of choice," that they were unnecessary and paternalistic, or that they interfered with the doctor-patient relationship. These objections ignore the concrete circumstances of how abuses happen and who most frequently suffers from them.

Postregulation statistics demonstrate a leveling of the rate of sterilization between Black and white women. This may be due in part to popular acceptance of the procedure as a method no longer reserved for the poor and disabled. Also, decreased spending power and pressures on white women to work outside the home are eroding social and economic differences between the middle class and the poor. A notable exception to this trend is recent New York City data which show that the percentage of procedures for Medicaid recipients is rising, with increasing disparities between white and Latin women (although this may be due to underreporting).

Current Issues in Sterilization

• *Reversal*

Today sterilization reversal is technically possible. Microsurgical procedures can reconnect a Fallopian tube or vas deferens severed during sterilization. But the rate of success is low, especially for those who are over 40 and have been sterilized for a considerable period of time by a method that destroys substantial tissue.

As a practical matter, reversal procedures are inaccessible to most people. Only a few large institutions offer this service, which is expensive (as much as $5,000 in 1987) and not usually covered by insurance. Some physicians will accept only married patients. Women who have undergone the surgery have an increased risk of ectopic pregnancy.

The apparent availability of reversal may lead to decisions to be sterilized by those who expect that it can be reversed later. Courts and government agencies may move away from their present stance and be more willing to permit sterilization of the poor or disabled if reversal is theoretically available, though no guarantee exists for funding of expensive reversal procedures.

• *AIDS*

As public attention has become focused on AIDS, there has been much discussion of compulsory testing of pregnant women or women at risk for AIDS to ascertain if they are HIV-positive. Because a woman with the HIV virus has a 30 to 50 percent chance of passing the infection to her children during gestation or birth, there is concern that abortion and sterilization will be recommended by counselors or that they will be involuntarily imposed by law. Since AIDS disproportionately affects Black and Latin communities, these possibilities are reminiscent of earlier population control campaigns that targeted women of color. There have always been apparently compelling arguments for compulsory sterilization but, as history demonstrates, the resulting sterilization abuse only avoided dealing with deeper social and economic issues.

Chapter 4

New Technologies and New Issues in Reproductive Control

For thousands of years, women have attempted to promote their fertility, as well as limit it. In early times, when fertility aids, like herbal brews, were simpler, women controlled their use and access. More modern technologies have a greater success rate, thus enhancing reproductive freedom. However, there are also disadvantages: High cost, inaccessability, side effects, and disappointment. Moreover, the increasing use of technology in the hands of the medical establishment has frightening implications for the future as women fight to retain autonomy over their reproductive lives.

Historically, a woman's worth was measured by her ability to bear children. A social stigma still attaches to childlessness, and relationships may fail because of it. Since the development of reproductive technologies in the late 1970s, the pressure on women to act in socially prescribed ways has been exploited by the often slim, highly expensive hope that they can become biological mothers through the new techniques. While some women have succeeded, the vast majority have suffered a profound sense of failure.

Infertility and Its Treatments

The media and the medical community would lead us to believe that infertility has become a problem of growing, even epidemic proportions when, in fact, the rate has been stable for the past 20 years. This propaganda is aimed at scaring women into early childbearing, at substantial cost to their work lives and autonomy, at a time when many women are deliberately postponing childbearing until their 30s and 40s when fertility is naturally lower. It conveniently ignores those factors responsible for real infertility—unsafe working conditions for both men and women; environmental pollution; side effects of the pill, IUD, DES (used until the 1970s to prevent miscarriage although totally ineffective for this purpose), and sexually transmitted diseases; sterilization abuse; inadequate health care in poor communities; and lack of gynecological care for lesbians.

The current overall figure of infertility is 8.5 percent of couples where the woman is between the ages of 15 and 44, though it is higher for Black and poor women. However, that statistic is highly questionable since it is based on "inability to conceive after one year of unprotected intercourse." In France, infertility is defined as inability to conceive after 2 years, which substantially reduces the resulting rate. If a couple has not conceived after one year of unprotected intercourse, they have a 49 percent chance of conceiving in the following year without treatment. Similarly, if they have been unable to conceive for 4 years, they have a 38 percent chance of conceiving spontaneously in the fifth year.

Therefore, the very definition of infertility used in the United States reveals a bias, motivated by the medical profession's desire to generate clients for its infertility services. In fact, there was little public discussion about infertility until the new techniques were developed. The marketing of these methods has raised expectations and created additional social pressures on women.

Alternative Insemination

Alternative insemination, sometimes known as the "turkey baster" method, involves depositing sperm in the vagina with a syringe. Not a high-tech procedure, it is especially useful for women without male partners and has become increasingly popular over the last 10 years.

When controlled by physicians and sperm banks, it becomes a highly oppressive technique and is called "artificial" insemination, thus reinforcing the notion that only heterosexual intercourse is "natural." Often charging high fees, such providers have the power to arbitrarily deny sperm to unmarried women, whether heterosexual or lesbian. Some sperm banks may reject married women whom they deem emotionally or financially unstable. Most sperm banks will only sell to doctors, so women are forced to depend on a physician or volunteer donors.

Because semen can carry dangerous viruses, including AIDS, women considering alternate insemination should consider the risk status of the donor. If there is any question, women should insist that the sperm donor be tested, the semen frozen, and the donor retested before insemination. Most sperm banks offer AIDS testing and genetic screening of donors, but thoroughness may vary greatly.

There may be legal questions involving alternative insemination. When sperm are donated to a bank, the donor relinquishes all parental rights to, and is relieved of responsibility for, any child conceived. But women who use more informal methods risk legal complications. In 1987 a California court awarded some parental rights to a man who had donated sperm to a lesbian couple.

In Vitro Fertilization

Since the introduction of in vitro fertilization (IVF), women have felt pressured to try it, even though the procedure is expensive, highly intrusive, and of limited success. About 1,000 IVF babies have been born in the United States since 1981, but success rates of programs vary widely. Of the approximately 150 centers that do IVF in the United States, nearly half had not achieved a live birth as of 1986.

IVF was developed as a treatment for women whose Fallopian tubes are blocked or missing. Blockage usually results from scarring due to pelvic inflammatory disease, often the result of using an IUD, or a sexually transmitted disease, severe endometriosis, or an earlier sterilization. Success rates vary depending on the cause of infertility, but most programs fail to note the differing success rates for different problems.

In IVF the woman's ovaries are stimulated with hormones to produce a number of eggs in a single cycle. The eggs are surgically removed, mixed with sperm, and if fertilized, they begin to divide. The resulting embryos are then transferred into the woman's uterus. If one or more of the embryos implant, the woman becomes pregnant.

In the most successful programs only about 10-12 percent of the women who begin a stimulation cycle will have a baby. Some will not ovulate; some will have no healthy eggs retrieved; some will have eggs that will not become fertilized or form embryos; many of the embryos will not implant; and about 30 percent of the pregnancies achieved will be miscarried. Because more than one embryo, if available, is transferred, there is a high rate of multiple births—about 30 percent in one relatively successful program.

There is a high rate of prematurity with IVF babies and a Cesarean section rate of 50 to 60 percent, even for single births. Some doctors will not transfer more than 4 embryos in a cycle, fearing the risks of a pregnancy with quintuplets or more. Others use selective abortion later in the pregnancy so that the woman will not face the health risk of bearing more than 3 or 4 babies.

Embryos can be frozen for implantation in a later cycle, sparing the woman repeated procedures. Such embryos can theoretically be used years later to produce a sibling, or they can be donated to a woman whose ovaries are missing or who carries a genetic disease. Frozen embryo implantation, however, is even less effective.

IVF clinics advertise misleading and inflated figures. Instead of counting every woman who begins taking the hormones, clinics note only those who have had an embryo transferred, thus doubling the "success rate." Also, instead of live births, they count pregnancies, despite the very large number that end in miscarriage. Most women in IVF programs have had several years of treatment, at least two prior operations, and many dashed hopes. Even though the chances of success diminish after 3 or 4 tries, some clinics will continue treatment indefinitely.

A simpler technique, called GIFT for "gamete intrafallopian transfer," has a somewhat higher success rate than does IVF for couples who have "infertility of unknown origin," that is, no diagnosable problem. Eggs are retrieved after stimulated ovulation, mixed with fresh sperm, and injected into the Fallopian tube where they presumably fertilize.

In vitro fertilization and most of the other techniques discussed here are rarely covered by insurance. They are very expensive: About $5,000 for one cycle of IVF or GIFT treatment and more for other techniques. The lack of coverage unfairly denies access to the poor and most of the middle class.

Contract Motherhood

Fertility sharing can be traced to the Biblical story of Sarah and Hagar, but the "Baby M" case brought contract motherhood into the headlines. Involving nothing more complicated by way of technology than alternative insemination, it is the commercialization of the procedure that raises controversial political, legal, and ethical questions. We use the term "contract" instead of "surrogate" motherhood because it emphasizes the legal arrangement for selling reproductive capacity and parental rights.

Contract motherhood has been heralded as the solution to a heterosexual couple's desire to have the man's biological child when he has fertile sperm and the woman is unable or unwilling to become pregnant. The couple contact a broker who finds a woman willing to produce a child for them for a fee. She contracts to be inseminated with the man's sperm, carry the resulting fetus to term, undergo amnio-centesis and abortion if the fetus is "imperfect," and surrender the baby and her parental rights to its biological father and his partner.

Many people object to the commercial nature of the relationship. In the "Baby M" case, for ex-ample, of the $25,000 fee paid, $10,000 went to the broker, $10,000 was alotted for the birth mother, and $5,000 covered medical expenses. To a poor woman, $10,000 may seem well worth 9 months of pregnancy with its many health risks. However, if she were paid the minimum hourly wage of $3.35 for 9 months, she would earn $63,000.

Contract motherhood, some argue, is baby selling, and selling a human, or the parental rights to a child, is prohibited by law. In the "Baby M" case, the lower court's decision that the biological father could enforce the contract and that the baby's mother had no rights was overturned on appeal. The New Jersey Supreme Court ruled in 1988 that the contract was unenforceable, that a woman could not contract away her right to maintain ties with her child before it was born, and that the adoption law, which always allows the birth mother to change her mind after the baby's birth, applies to such cases. Ultimately, custody was granted to the biological father, but the birth mother received substantial visitation rights.

State legislatures are also dealing with the issue. As of October 1988, 4 states had passed laws making such contracts void and unenforceable; 2 state statutes permitted the arrangement, but only with strict judicial review; and 20 state legislatures were considering laws to regulate or prohibit the practice.

There are other forms of contract motherhood that are technologically, as well as legally, even more complex. One is called the "gestational surrogate," "surrogate womb," or "guest womb." After an embryo is produced in vitro, using an egg and sperm from the couple wanting the child, the embryo or embryos are transferred into a woman who has contracted to carry the fetus or fetuses to term. This technique has an even lower success rate than ordinary IVF because embryos are less likely to implant in the uterus of an unrelated woman. The technique also requires an exquisite and prolonged synchronization of the two women's cycles so that the recipient's uterus is at the proper stage to receive the embryo.

Commercial contract motherhood procedures raise the spectre of poor women renting their wombs to the more affluent. Where the form of contract motherhood requires the woman's genetic contribution, it is feared that women of color will not be selected. Conversely, there is

Elizabeth Catlett

widespread fear that with gestational surrogacy women of color will be particularly exploited. There are many debates among feminists and in the progressive community about contract motherhood. It may well be that what is objectionable is the commercial nature of the relationship and that when women share fertility without financial exchange (for example, a friend or relative bearing a child for another woman), women may be empowered and reproductive freedom advanced.

Prenatal Testing and Genetic Screening

As prenatal testing for possible birth defects has become commonplace, it has raised people's expectations of having the "perfect baby." The availability of techniques may make mothers feel guilty if they were not tested and had less-than-perfect babies. Poor prenatal nutrition, unforeseen events during labor and delivery, and accidents after birth—not genetic problems—cause most cases of brain damage, mental or developmental retardation, and conditions such as cerebral palsy.

Prenatal tests can predict the occurrence of several hundred chromosomal conditions, notably Downs syndrome and Tay-Sachs disease, and of neural tube defects, such as spina bifida and anencepha-ly. Unfortunately, prenatal testing is far from perfect. Mistakes are made; some conditions are not screened for; test results are sometimes difficult or impossible to interpret; and no one knows the long-term effects of testing on the fetus. Yet today prenatal testing is recommended for all women over 35, and as the technology advances, women as young as 30 may feel obligated to be tested.

Testing is recommended for couples who have already had a child with a chromosomal condition or where one partner may be a carrier of an abnormality. If the woman is, for any reason, reluctant to have the procedure, she may face considerable pressure from her doctor, her family, or her friends. On the other hand, people at risk for genetic complications might not become pregnant or might abort if they could not test each pregnancy for the presence of disabling conditions.

Three prenatal tests are widely available. The most frequently used is amniocentesis, performed between 12 and 16 weeks of pregnancy. The fetus and placenta are located by ultrasound, amniotic fluid is drawn out of a woman's uterus through a needle, and fetal cells are then tested. If the fetus is found to have a disabling condition, the woman then has the option of a second-trimester abortion. The risk of miscarriage caused by amniocentesis is about 3 in 1,000.

A newer procedure called chorionic villi sampling (CVS) can be done as early as the eighth week of pregnancy, although it is usually performed between weeks 9 and 10. A thin catheter, inserted into the uterus through the cervix, draws out cells from the membrane surrounding the amniotic sac, which are then tested. Because results are obtained sooner than with amniocentesis, a woman may have an early abortion.

The miscarriage rate following CVS ranges from 2 to 10 percent above the normal miscarriage rate (depending on provider experience), though as the procedure is done more routinely, the rates should become lower. Since some abnormalities may cause spontaneous early abortion, some of the miscarriages following CVS might have occurred naturally.

Both amniocentesis and CVS require ultrasound, which uses high-frequency sound waves. Although ultrasound is used today as a diagnostic procedure in most pregnancies, its long-term effects are unknown. This raises concern because X-rays were performed on pregnant women for more than 30 years before the relationship between X-rays and childhood leukemia and other cancers was recognized.

The third prenatal test, the maternal alpha-fetoprotein test (AFP), uses the mother's blood to diagnose neural tube defects in the fetus. There is no risk to the fetus or the pregnancy from the test itself, but because AFP is done at 16 weeks, a second-trimester abortion would be necessary to terminate the pregnancy.

Aside from the risks of miscarriage caused by amniocentesis and CVS, there may be emotional or ethical problems for women, which are rarely recognized or acknowledged by doctors or counselors. Many women find the procedures painful, invasive, and disturbing. Women may have difficulty committing themselves to a pregnancy they fear they may end up aborting. Few women are warned of the possibility of an ambiguous test result. Because results do not reveal the severity of an abnormality, women cannot make an informed choice and may feel compelled to unnecessarily abort. An abortion is often especially emotionally difficult when the baby is otherwise wanted.

With CVS and amniocentesis it is possible to know the sex of the fetus. While there has been some fear that people might abort fetuses because of their sex, that seems not to be a frequent occurrence in the United States. In India, however, where amniocentesis costs $8 (compared with about $800 here), a study of 8,000 fetuses aborted after amniocentesis found that 7,999 of them were female.

The expectation of the "perfect baby" acts to reinforce people's prejudices against people with disabilities. The disability rights movement fears that if it becomes unacceptable for a woman to carry a fetus with a minor genetic condition to term, disabled people will become even more isolated and stigmatized. Since social and economic conditions, as well as bigoted attitudes, pose the main barriers to the disabled, ensuring rights for the disabled and their families is essential. The same lack of social and other services may discourage a woman from having a child who is known to have a genetic condition for fear that she will be unable to properly care for such a child.

Fetal Surgery and Childbirth Technology

Intrauterine procedures to treat fetuses are at a very experimental stage, but research is occurring and techniques are being developed that may some day save lives. Neonatal intensive care is routinely used to save premature babies.

The growing use of technology and surgery in labor and delivery has, however, markedly decreased women's control of childbirth. Childbirth preparation classes, the resurgence of midwifery, and the presence of partners in the labor room have in no way reversed the trend toward doctor-managed birth. For instance, fetal monitoring has become routine in the majority of hospitals. While it has benefits, the number of cases in which it is needed is limited, and it may actually cause complications. Because a woman must lie on her back, which restricts the supply of blood to the placenta and fetus, using a fetal monitor may lead to a Cesarean delivery, which might otherwise not have been needed.

The Cesarean section rate, about 25 percent nationally, but nearer 40 percent in some hospitals, has risen steadily over the past 15 years. Doctors claim they perform Cesareans because of their fear of malpractice suits. Although this is a real concern, studies show that most Cesarean sections occur in the late afternoon and early morning. One possible explanation is that doctors do Cesareans so they can get home for dinner or to clear operating and labor rooms for the day shift.

Women have been ordered by courts to undergo fetal surgery and Cesarean section or face charges of child abuse. In two such cases, the women fled and later delivered healthy babies vaginally. In 1987, in shocking disregard for the rights of a dying patient, a Washington, D.C., judge ordered a woman to undergo a Cesarean to "save" a 21-week fetus. Both mother and baby died soon afterwards. When a court compels a woman to undergo any procedure, medical or surgical, against her will for the benefit of the fetus she carries, the court denies her humanity and autonomy, viewing her instead simply as a vessel that must be made ideal for the baby-to-be.

The money now spent on new techniques would help a greater number of people if it were invested in the nonglamorous tasks of improving the nutrition of pregnant women, lowering the high infant mortality rate in poor Black and Latin communities, preventing or eliminating environmental causes of infertility, or encouraging the adoption of existing babies. A national health system would not only prevent much of the social and economic causes of infertility, but could also make the new technologies available on a more rational basis. Real reproductive freedom involves both access to women-controlled means of promoting fertility and freeing women from the oppressive expectations of compulsory motherhood and social prejudice against women who are not mothers.

Chapter 5

Abortion in the Courts: What Rights Do Women Really Have?

Beginning in the late 19th century, individual states made it a crime to perform or have an abortion. These were the laws that were under attack in the struggle for "free abortion on demand" which began in the late 1960s. Although the struggle occurred on many fronts, the legislatures and the courts became a main focus. In 1967 advocates won a small victory: the state of Colorado passed a law allowing abortion up to the 16th week of pregnancy if a doctor agreed that carrying to term would endanger the physical and emotional health of the woman, or if there was a suspicion of fetal abnormality. Abortion was also allowed for women whose pregnancies resulted from rape or incest. Hawaii was next in 1970, but a 90-day residency requirement was imposed. Later that year, New York liberalized its law without imposing restrictions or a residency requirement, and the state became a mecca for women choosing to end a pregnancy.

At the time, groups like population control agencies and the American Medical Association also exerted political pressure for legal abortion as part of their general aims to contain population growth and increase their control over reproduction. Not surprisingly, these groups focused their efforts on the courts.

Many legal cases challenged the constitutionality of statutes criminalizing abortion, and in 1973 the Supreme Court finally decided the abortion question in the landmark case of *Roe v. Wade*. Although the decision was hailed as a revolutionary affirmation of women's rights, its reasoning also set the framework for legislative attempts to limit women's ability to obtain abortions ever since. To understand the present legal situation of both abortion and the general "right to privacy," it is important to understand exactly what the Court did and did not hold in *Roe v. Wade.*

The *Roe v. Wade* Decision

The Supreme Court's decision was hardly the unqualified acknowledgment of a woman's right to abortion for which feminists had hoped. Although the Court decided that the fetus is not a "person" for constitutional purposes, it recognized only the limited right of a woman to "choose," with the aid of her doctor, to terminate her pregnancy free from unwarranted governmental interference. The right that is protected is not *having* an abortion, but *choosing* to have one, a difference that became significant in subsequent cases dealing with government funding of abortion. Moreover, the Court found the abortion decision was "in all its aspects—inherently and primarily, a medical decision," and thus the choice was, at least in part, the *doctor's.* Without a doctor's willingness to perform it, there could be no abortion.

Another key limitation was that the courts would intervene only when the state placed an "unwarranted" or "unjustified" burden on the abortion decision. This determination was to be made weighing the state's interest in the regulation against the woman's choice, based on the length of her pregnancy.

The Court found that although the fetus itself has no rights, the state has an interest in the "preservation or protection" of "potential human life." This interest becomes compelling—that is, the state may restrict or remove a woman's choice subject only to her life or health—after the fetus becomes "viable." At the time *Roe* was decided, viability was around 28 weeks, or at the beginning of the third trimester of pregnancy. Since then, advances in medical technology have pushed viability back to 24 weeks and may continue to decrease the period in which the woman's choice or health overrules the state's interest in protecting potential human life.

The Court ruled that the state could also infringe on the abortion choice to protect maternal health. Although this interest does not become "compelling" until the end of the first trimester, after that time the Court will uphold regulations that are reasonably related to maternal health. Subsequent cases have determined that restrictions or regulations consistent with generally accepted medical practice will be considered "reasonable" within this test. *Roe* thus linked the abortion decision not only to medical control and medically determined health considerations, but also recognized the legitimacy of the state's interest in "encouraging childbirth" to promote potential human life.

These aspects of *Roe v. Wade* were and are understood by anti-choice groups as potential ways to severely limit—if they could not directly outlaw—women's choice of abortion. Immediately following *Roe*, they repeatedly went to state and local legislatures, as well as to Congress, seeking restrictions consistent with the state interests discussed in that case. The following years saw continuing legal battles about the constitutionality of such restrictions.

Varieties of State Regulation

The state laws enacted to restrict abortion met with some success and some defeat. They included restrictions in the following categories:

• *Medicalization Regulations*

These include laws that restrict performance of second trimester abortion to hospitals rather than doctors' offices or free standing clinics. The effect of such laws, which have generally been upheld for abortions other than D and Es done before the 16th week, is to dramatically increase the cost of abortion, placing it beyond the reach of many women. Since many hospitals do not perform abortions, rural women have to travel great distances to find a hospital that does provide services, thus adding to both the cost and difficulty of exercising their "abortion choice."

• *Reporting Requirements*

These include laws that require filing reports on all abortions, including confidential information about both the pregnant woman and the abortion provider. A relatively simple statistical reporting requirement was upheld as a legitimate health measure shortly after *Roe v. Wade*, but the purpose of more recently enacted requirements seems quite different. A Pennsylvania provision included information available to the general public on request, with no real medical benefits. A bare majority of the Court understood the risk of identification that might result in harassment or threats to the woman or the possibility of bombings or other violence against an unadvertised provider and struck down the statute in 1986.

• *"Informed Consent" Regulations*

The law provides that a person who considers any kind of medical treatment should be given sufficient information about the potential risks and benefits, possible side effects, and consequences of the treatment to make an informed choice. Anti-abortion legislators have distorted and abused this general principle by requiring a pregnant woman to be lectured on the development of her "unborn child," shown pictures of fetuses at various stages, and be told about the availability of adoption and adoption-related services. Statutes have also mandated false information, for example, that "abortion is a major surgical procedure" with "numerous possible physical and psychological consequences."

Again, a bare majority of the Court held that mandating such information is not to inform, but to improperly influence a woman's choice against abortion. The Court also held that mandating such information is an unconstitutional "intrusion on the discretion of the pregnant woman's physician."

• *Substituted Consent Regulation*

A number of states have passed laws requiring that the husband of a married woman or the parents of a minor must give prior consent to a woman's abortion. The Court has rejected spousal consent, but has upheld parental notification for unemancipated minors living at home, finding a special state interest in promoting "family integrity." The real impact of these statutes, however, is to discourage young women from having abortions by making that choice more difficult. Because of this extra burden, teenagers will have later abortions, which are more haz-

Doug Barnes/Guardian photo

ardous, and may be subjected to abuse or violence if their parents learn of their pregnancies.

Thus far, the Court has addressed these problems by mandating "judicial bypass"—a way for a young woman to get the consent of a court without ever approaching her parents. This bypass presents its own difficulties for a young, frightened pregnant woman.

• *Post-Viability Provisions*

In a late abortion, after the fetus is considered viable, states have passed, and the Court has upheld, laws requiring the presence of a second doctor whose sole function is to preserve the fetus' life. This adds enormously to the cost of the abortion, making it effectively unavailable to many women. It may also involve a great psychological burden for the woman who experiences the trauma of a live birth followed by infant mortality. Since most late abortion techniques do not involve the possibility of a live birth, this requirement serves no state interest in the majority of cases.

In addition, states have passed laws requiring a doctor to choose the procedure most likely to result in a live birth. So far such laws have been held unconstitutional if the means chosen poses a greater threat to the woman's life or health than a procedure in which there is no possibility of fetal survival.

• *Defunding*

The most effective limitation on abortion to date has come from laws like the Hyde Amendment that prohibit the use of Medicaid funds for poor women's abortions. Prior to 1977 when the Hyde Amendment was first passed, nearly 295,000 women per year had abortions paid for by federal Medicaid funds. Following the cutoff, many poor women have been faced with increasingly difficult choices: 80 percent scrape together the money for an abortion at enormous cost to themselves and their families, or resort to illegal or self-induced abortions; and 20 percent give birth. Though there are no studies to document it, many of these women then "choose" sterilization, which the government fully funds, as the only certain fertility control available to them.

Many state legislatures have also prohibited the use of state monies for abortions. As of 1988 only 14 states (Alaska, California, Connecticut, Hawaii, Massachusetts, Michigan, New Jersey, New York, North Carolina, Oregon, Rhode Island, Vermont, Washington, West Virginia) and the District of Columbia still fund abortions. Other legislation has barred municipal hospitals from providing abortion services (private hospitals have been subjected to these restrictions).

The Court has consistently upheld statutes that deny abortions to tens of thousands of poor women. The defunding tactic is based directly on *Roe v. Wade*. Because the Court ruled that there is no right to *have* an abortion, government has no obligation to pay for abortions. It may elect to pay for childbirth, but not pregnancy termination, even if the woman's life or health is endangered. In its decisions the Court has completely ignored the blatantly discriminatory impact on poor women.

The "New" Court and the Future of Abortion Rights

There are nine Justices on the Supreme Court, and when *Roe v. Wade* was decided, eight of them voted in favor of the "right to choose." Since 1973, a number have retired and been replaced by more conservative, Reagan-appointed Justices including Sandra Day O'Connor, the first woman on the Court. Only four of the original *Roe* majority are still on the Court, and many believe a serious retreat from *Roe* is imminent.

After Lewis Powell retired in 1987, Reagan nominated Judge Robert Bork, who stated that the Constitution contains no protection for a woman's choice of abortion, along with other highly conservative views. As a result of a broad grassroots campaign by feminists, civil libertarians, civil rights, and pro-choice organizations, the nomination was withdrawn. Judge Anthony Kennedy, who was finally confirmed, is not so blatantly anti-abortion as Bork, but he is not expected to defend the right to choose.

A new trend, which Kennedy will likely endorse, can be best seen in the opinions of Sandra Day O'Connor. O'Connor does not explicitly call for overturning *Roe v. Wade*, as Chief Justice Rehnquist has. Instead she argues for a more limited judicial review and greater deference to laws passed by state legislators and Congress. She would consider the state's interest in preserving potential human life as equally important throughout pregnancy, not just at viability. She also believes the Court should uphold legislation that limits, but does not absolutely prohibit, abortion as long as there is any reasonable basis. She would also uphold restrictions (such as the hospitalization requirements or "informed consent" anti-abortion propaganda) which do not place a *substantial* burden on a woman's choice.

If O'Connor's views prevail, abortion may not be illegal, but obtaining one will be more and more difficult, expensive, and dangerous.

For many women—poor, young, living in rural or more isolated areas, or with unwanted pregnancies in later stages—abortion may simply be unavailable, though it may technically not be illegal. The real right to free abortion on demand—first heard over 20 years ago, but never accepted by the legal system—recedes further and further from judicial acceptance, much less constitutional protection.

Understanding the Limitations of the Courts

The courts, and particularly the Supreme Court, are highly political institutions, responding to a variety of forces including a powerful backlash against gains made by women in all aspects of society. A powerful, organized women's movement is needed to continue the essential though limited protection the courts have afforded us. However, the courts are only one arena in which the struggle for reproductive freedom must be waged.

Chapter 6

Changing Social and Economic Conditions: New Opportunities, Old Burdens

Today, family and household structures are changing rapidly. Some view this as a crisis, calling it the "decay of civilization," while others believe it is a change long overdue. Feminists, aware of the continuing oppression based on sex, race, and sexual orientation, demand even greater changes.

Those who are threatened by changes in "the family" blame them on the feminist, lesbian/gay, welfare rights, and civil rights movements. Women's struggle for legal abortion is a favorite target of the right wing. Unfortunately, many sincere people, motivated by religious and moral beliefs, have been swept along with this reactionary upsurge (discussed in Chapter 7). Many women's legitimate fears about the security of their marriages and their children's future may be exploited by the right wing. This chapter will discuss the sweeping social changes in families within this context.

Women's Changing Role at Work and at Home

The single most significant indicator of change is that fewer than one-fifth of American families fit the father-breadwinner, mother-housewife model. Today 55 percent of mothers with children under 6 are in the labor force, nearly 3 times their number in 1960. In 1985, 51.5 million women workers, who were 54.5 percent of all U.S. females, accounted for 44.2 percent of the workforce. But just as in the 1950s, women are still primarily responsible for childrearing and running the household, although some men are sharing household chores and "helping" with the kids.

The increase in women working outside the home is due both to women's rising expectations for themselves and to a declining standard of living. Because of a general assault on wages, extensive takebacks in benefits, and massive layoffs in heavy industry, working people have experienced a sharp decline in purchasing power since the late 1970s. Workers' real wages are now below 1963 levels. Seven out of 10 working mothers say they must work to make ends meet—not to get ahead and not because the women's movement encouraged them to work outside the home.

Because mothers of children under 6 are the fastest growing category of new workers, childcare has become a wrenching problem for millions of women, each struggling to find an individual solution. Statistics show that in 1986, 9 million preschoolers were cared for by someone other than their mothers.

Another major change is that one quarter of all families are headed by single women. This number represents a jump of 82 percent since 1970. Seventy percent of these mothers work, yet one-third of these families live in poverty. Over half of Black female-headed families remain poor.

In 1986 one out of 4 children lived in a single-parent home. Among white children 18 percent lived with one parent, compared with 30 percent of Latin children and 53 percent of Black children. Nearly 2 of every 3 children will live in a single-parent household at some time before adulthood.

The rise in the number of households headed by single women is one cause of a phenomenon that was recognized in the 1980s: The feminization of poverty. Households headed by single women account for 75 percent of the poor. Forty percent of that number are children, even though children are only 27 percent of the population. Almost half of all Black children and more than one-third of Latin children live in poverty. Women are 71 percent of the poor over age 65. Older women and women with children are joining the homeless in great numbers.

Several economic factors, reflecting the profound sexism and racism in society, account for the feminization of poverty (in addition to the fact that men increasingly feel free to abandon their families). Other factors are that full-time women workers are paid on the average 64 cents for every dollar a man makes. While white women make 60 percent of white men's wages, Black women 76 percent of Black men's, and Latin women 73 percent of Latin men's, Black women earn 54 percent of what white men make. Although some women are entering professions and lower echelons of management, the vast majority are segregated in women's traditional, low-paying service jobs: 80 percent of all women are employed in only 20 of the Bureau of Labor Statistics' 427 job classifications. Of jobs being created in the 1980s, 80 percent are in retail sales and services where average wages, when adjusted for inflation, fall below the average national wage in 1949.

Workers World Photo

Daycare demonstration

Millions of women are also trapped by socioeconomic Catch 22s. Women who receive welfare and Medicaid can only find low-paying jobs, with no benefits, and so cannot earn enough money to support their families and pay for childcare and medical care. Therefore, many women "choose" to stay on welfare until their children are in school. Divorce almost always worsens a woman's economic situation. Statistics show that a divorced woman's standard of living is reduced over 40 percent, while her former husband's rises over 70 percent. Thus, economic need forces many women to remain in bad marriages rather than face impoverishment. Because Social Security benefits and pensions are based on earnings and years worked, women who left work to raise children and/or worked in low-paying jobs often become destitute in later years.

While these statistics indicate that single women as a group are economically worse off, there are other, contrary indications of positive social change for single women. Many women are choosing to delay marriage until they gain work experience or establish careers. Some women are choosing to be single mothers, with lesbian families and 2 single-mother households also increasing.

There are other indicators of change as well. For instance, more teenagers are sexually active; more lesbians and gay men are visibly "out"; more unmarried couples, both lesbian/gay and straight, live together openly; and more married couples are delaying having children. Because nearly half of all marriages end in divorce, there are growing numbers of "blended" families, with his, hers, and their children raised together. This also includes families where both parents are lesbian or gay. Stepparenting may provide an opportunity to expand the notion of what constitutes a family.

Working outside the home has boosted many women's self-esteem and shifted the balance of power between husbands and wives, often giving women more leverage within their marriages. But most women are not happier. Women find that men expect them to earn a living and still play traditional nurturing, loving roles. Women say men try to control them by coercive emotional violence—insults, hostility, teasing, or aggressive behavior. Half the 50,000 respondents to a 1987 *Family Circle* survey said that today they would not choose to marry their husbands again.

Why Challenges to the Traditional Family Provoked a Backlash

These changes coupled with more liberal attitudes about equality, sexuality, virginity, divorce, being unmarried, and growing old are inconsistent with the traditional patriarchial order. Increased awareness and pressure from the feminist movement have stigmatized such behavior as battering and abuse, marital rape, incest, and child molestation, which were always present in the patriarchial family. (However, there is no national system of safe homes, sanctuaries, or transitional housing in every community to offer abused women a real alternative.) Still, all these factors undermine individual male dominance at the same time as women's status and economic power are growing. They also create an opening for women to expand their familial role.

Rather than viewing some of these changes as moves toward more egalitarian, honest, and pleasurable social relations, right-wing forces have responded with fear and rage, singling out legal abortion as their primary target. Women gaining even minimal control over their bodies has proven to be too much of a threat to their authoritarian goals, prompting the anti-abortion crusade, with its lies, deception, and violence.

By playing on people's fears and promoting their prejudices, the New Right created a backlash that led, in part, to 8 years of Reaganite reaction. How did the "pro-family" administration respond? By making massive cuts in social services—school lunches, food stamps, prenatal and postnatal nutritional supplements for women, infants, and children (WIC), welfare grants, job training and education, and public housing.

Between fiscal 1982 and 1985, for instance, $5 billion was cut from school lunch, breakfast, and summer food programs. Food

stamps were cut by $6.8 billion during the same period, reducing benefits for 18 million people.

In 1986 not a single state provided a welfare grant equal to the poverty level! In fact, one grassroots welfare movement is called "Up to Poverty." In 1987 one in 6 children had no health insurance and lived in a household where no adult had a job. Virtually no federal funding has been allocated to build new public housing since 1981, despite epidemic homelessness.

Since the early 1980s, federal funding for daycare for low- and middle-income families has been cut by 28 percent, and 23 states are providing childcare to fewer children than in 1981. The United States is alone among 100 industrialized countries in having no national system of childcare, guaranteed paid parental leave, or pre- and postnatal health care. Even a poor country like Nicaragua guarantees women 3 months' maternity leave, the right to return to their jobs, and daily childcare.

At the same time that cuts were made in social programs, $67 billion went to fund the Strategic Defense Initiative ("Star Wars") and the military budget skyrocketed to over $200 billion a year. According to the 1988 budget put out by the Children's Defense Fund: "A single hour's global military expenditure could save 3.5 million children from preventable infectious diseases and ten days ($500 million) of the proposed Pentagon increase for [fiscal 1988] could provide prenatal care to thousands." What has occurred is a massive transfer of funds from needed social services to destructive military uses. Not only is this a huge drain on the economy, resulting in an astronomical national debt, but it also depletes human resources needed for a vital society. Such social policy promotes poverty and homelessness, which ironically may pressure poor women to seek abortions.

Another aspect of the "pro-family" backlash was the defeat of the Equal Rights Amendment (ERA), whose opponents included big business and the military. But that was no coincidence. This backlash is *anti-feminist:* a reaction against women's ability to live on their own as workers and mothers by trying to keep them dependent on individual men and/or the state. For as long as women suffer job discrimination and are paid only two-thirds of what men make for the same work, and as long as women do not have effective means to control their fertility, they will be forced to remain dependent on a male "supporter." Reactionary forces are counting on this to undercut the influence of the women's movement.

There is another reason for this backlash. Despite the stock market boom of the mid-1980s, the general decrease in the standard of living and the massive cuts in heavy industry provide an economic context for the growth of the right wing. While all levels of government have cut back essential social services—hospitals, schools, senior centers, libraries—these cutbacks affect all working people by eliminating jobs, lowering the floor on wages and putting additional strain on Social Security, pension funds, and unemployment benefits. They affect women by adding greatly to the traditional burden of caring for children, the ill, the elderly, and the unemployed.

Attacking abortion rights and scapegoating women plays into this attempt to manipulate, obscure, and sidetrack people's understanding of the causes of the economic crisis. Yet despite the right wing's attempts in the 1980s, this backward divide-and-conquer ideology has not been entirely successful. Blaming the victim is not persuasive when large numbers of people in the idled factory towns of Ohio, the foreclosed farms in Nebraska, and the once-booming sunbelt are in need.

While anti-feminism and anti-abortionism are central to the right wing's social agenda, women's increasingly visible, always indispensable role in society—as both workers and caretakers—is raising women's feminist consciousness. A 1986 poll in *Newsweek* found that 65 percent of Black women and 56 percent of white women consider themselves feminists. This is a fitting rebuke to the right wing and reason for optimism in the years ahead.

Chapter 7

Challenging Political Backlash from the Right

The legalization of abortion in 1973 affirmed the feminist movement's overall objective of freeing women from oppressive governmental, social, and religious restraints on reproductive choice. Yet, for all that *Roe v. Wade* encouraged women, the right wing understood its implications. The backlash began in earnest.

Already panicked by gains won by the civil rights movement, the impending loss of the war in Vietnam, and what they called a general breakdown of "law and order," conservatives began forming single-issue groups against busing, desegregation, sex education, the ERA, lesbian and gay rights, and abortion. As these groups coalesced during the 1970s, their politics came to be called the "New Right."

One of the New Right's ideologues, Paul Weyrich of the Committee for Survival of a Free Congress, revealed the purpose of this conservative agenda: "We talk about issues people care about, like gun control, abortion, taxes, and crime. Yes, they're emotional issues, but that's better than talking about capital formation." Thus the New Right distanced itself from the elitist ideology and practice of the conservatives generally aligned with the Republican Party by appealing to ordinary peoples' vulnerability and feelings of powerlessness.

Opposing women's control over their lives took the moral guise of saving "innocent life" and "the family." Their rhetoric is deceptive; they claim to be "pro-life," all the while supporting nuclear arms, the death penalty, and funding cuts in social service programs. This manipulation of language was key to sanitizing and sanctifying its overall strategy. The *Roe* decision provided the issue the New Right needed to galvanize its anti-woman, especially anti-feminist, backlash.

Church Efforts Merge with the New Right

The anti-abortion movement got a significant boost, if not its official start, from the well-organized Catholic Church, which turned the anti-abortion cause into a modern day crusade. So clear was the connection, that members of the National Right to Life Committee (NRTL), fearing the political implications of a Catholic-dominated movement, voted to become independent of the U.S. Catholic Conference in June 1973. The NRTL still relies, however, on Catholic Conference funds for its operation.

Individual Catholics, like New York's Cardinal Cooke, spoke for the crusade. They were soon joined by Protestants like Dr. J.C. Wilkie, who became President of NRTL after heading a Michigan anti-abortion campaign of 8,000 volunteers in 1972 called "Voice of the Unborn." Wilkie described his tactics, which became bywords for the crusade: "Never use the words fetus or embryo. Use baby. Always use the word kill."

During a rally in Washington, D.C. on the first anniversary of the *Roe* decision, thousands of Catholic churchgoers joined with members of newly formed anti-abortion and right-wing single-issue groups to demand an amendment to the U.S. Constitution protecting life from the moment of conception. Soon many right-wing groups began organizing with a vengeance. Conservative think tanks such as the Heritage Foundation published journals and op-ed pieces in major newspapers that created an ideological framework for the right-wing electoral sweep of 1980. Strategic coalitions were formed. Overlapping boards of directors, with people from the New Right as well as single-issue anti-abortion groups, became common.

Fundamentalist Protestant groups, like the Moral Majority and PTL (Praise The Lord) Club, were part of the right-wing coalition boom. By 1981, the Rev. Jerry Falwell, one of the most vociferous fundamentalist leaders, was watched by 50 million people on 324 TV stations in the United States, Canada, and the Caribbean. He constantly admonished viewers to "end the biological holocaust of unborn babies" and plugged the dogma that "life begins at the moment of conception."

The Roman Catholic Church was operating politically alongside these rightists. By 1976 the National Conference of Catholic Bishops had organized an anti-abortion group in every congressional district. In the "Pastoral Plan for Pro-Life Activities," the bishops urged Roman Catholics to move out "into society" by engaging in anti-abortion work.

In 1977 all these organizing efforts resulted in passage of the Hyde Amendment, which in turn intensified political activity. That year the

National Committee for a Human Life Amendment formed, with $270,000 from dioceses around the country, and both Catholic and fundamentalist churches became visible in electoral politics.

By the time of the 1980 elections, every Catholic and fundamentalist churchgoer in America knew that Republican presidential candidate Ronald Reagan was anti-choice, anti-gay/lesbian rights, anti-sex education in the schools, and anti-ERA. Although the Catholic Church did not officially endorse him, the faithful were primed. When Reagan won, emboldened anti-choice Catholics joined forces with fundamentalists and New Right activists and geared up, in the words of Life Amendment Political Action Committee Director Paul Brown, "to haunt to death" pro-choice members of Congress by running well-funded, highly organized electoral compaigns, which unseated some of them.

On the ninth anniversary of *Roe*, 3 days after being sworn in as President, Reagan met with delegates of the anti-abortion movement. Soon he began appointing women and men allied with a panoply of right-wing social issues. Within months, hundreds of anti-abortion bills and constitutional amendments were introduced in Congress, 16 in the first week alone. But before addressing these attacks, it is important to look at how the reproductive rights movement fought the anti-abortion legislation after *Roe*.

Countering Legislative and Constitutional Attacks

Within 9 months of the *Roe* decision, 188 bills to restrict abortion were introduced in 41 states. As described in Chapter 5, post-*Roe* statutes included requirements of spousal or parental consent, hospitalization for second trimester abortions, mandatory waiting periods, and funding restrictions.

In 1977 Congress passed the Hyde Amendment, cutting off federal Medicaid funding for abortions for poor women. Peace Corps volunteers, military and Defense Department personnel, and federal workers and their dependents had their insurance coverage for abortion eliminated between 1978 and 1979.

In response to the escalating attacks on abortion rights, pro-choice groups mobilized. Established groups such as Planned Parenthood and NARAL (National Abortion Rights Action League) engaged in media campaigns, lobbying, and educational work. They also took cases into court, challenging laws restricting abortion. Activist feminists formed new organizations. From coast to coast, groups like CARASA in New York City and Buffalo, and the Committee to Defend Reproductive

Rights in San Francisco, petitioned, lobbied, and tabled; held street meetings, speakouts, and conferences; and demonstrated in protest.

The first national fightback campaign was "Abortion Rights Action Week" in 1979 in which over 80 cities participated with 200 activities. By 1981, 80 organizations had coalesced to form the Reproductive Rights National Network (R2N2), with affiliates in England and Australia. Abortion Rights Action Week and other protests succeeded: Many restrictions introduced in state legislatures and Congress did not pass or were ruled unconstitutional.

While the number of federally-funded Medicaid abortions plummeted from 295,000 in 1977 to about 3,000 in 1986, 14 states (see Chapter 5) and the District of Columbia continue to fund Medicaid abortions wholly out of local revenue. Five others pay for abortions for rape and incest victims, women at risk of having a deformed child, or women for whom having a child is life endangering. In 1985 over 188,000 women were able to have state-funded Medicaid abortions, thanks in large part to organizing and lobbying by pro-choice activists. Still, 32 states, including the entire central and southern regions, provide no coverage unless a woman's life is threatened by a nine-month pregnancy.

Nevertheless, it is significant that none of the hundreds of other proposed anti-abortion state constitutional amendments passed. Nor did an attempt to call a U.S. Constitutional Convention for the purpose of adding an anti-abortion amendment. Despite heavy organizing for a convention, only 19 of the needed 34 states have requested one to date, and some of these have since been withdrawn.

The reproductive rights movement mobilized to counter these reactionary moves. Activists demonstrated at NRTL offices and countered anti-abortionists at every turn with a visible, vocal presence. In April 1981, 6 members of the Women's Liberation Zap Action Brigade disrupted congressional hearings on the so-called "Human Life Statute" to protest that the hearings were skewed in favor of anti-abortionists.

Although feminist activity was important in defeating these amendments, women's interests were not the sole motivating force. A number of disparate, often contradictory forces also opposed radical constitutional change. These included the population control establishment, such as Zero Population Growth and the Rockefeller-funded Population Council. Other organizations like Planned Parenthood typify some of the contradictory forces: They are advocates for women's interests, but they push population control, particularly sterilization, in the Third World. Even some conservative lawmakers could not support a Constitutional Convention whose agenda was to dismantle the Bill of Rights. Another factor was disunity in the anti-abortion movement, which was demoralized by defeats in the courts. Its leaders were divided over whether to endorse a constitutional amendment declaring that life begins at conception or one that would allow each state to decide when or if abortion was permissible.

Harassment, A New Tactic

Tired of whittling away at choice, anti-abortion activists wanted to ban it outright. According to the president of Catholics United for Life, "People with the stick-to-itiveness to be involved in a movement like this...want more activity, more radical thinking." Groups like Joe Scheidler's Chicago--based Pro-Life Action League and the Pearson Foundation gave the cause a new focus away from the legislative, electoral arena.

David Vita/Impact Visuals

Bomb-damaged waiting room at the Eastern Women's Center Abortion Clinic, New York City, October 29, 1986.

By 1982 anti-abortionists stepped up "sidewalk counseling" designed to frighten women from entering abortion clinics. Their methods are shrill—taunts of "babykiller" are typical—and they carry bottled fetuses or pictures of bloody, dismembered body parts to make their point. Doctors who perform abortions and clinic staff have been subjected to crank calls and death threats. Women leaving clinics have been berated, followed, and threatened.

Clinic "invasions"—the unlawful intrusion into a clinic to stage a sit-down protest—became frequent. So did violence against clinics. The greatest number of incidents was in 1984. There were 150 disruptions, including the machine gunning of Ladies First Choice Medical Group in Pembroke Pines, Florida. There were also 29 bomb and arson attacks and 5 instances of extreme vandalism. In 1985 there were 21 bomb or arson attacks or attempts, 3 instances of extreme vandalism (for example, gunshots fired through a window in the home of Supreme Court Justice Harry Blackmun, principal author of *Roe v. Wade*), and 3 assaults. In 1986 the number was similar, marked only by the fact that for the first time a bomb was placed in a building known to be occupied.

The reproductive rights movement responded by rallying to the clinics' defense. Weekly counterpickets and "escort services" have been organized. Pro-choice women and men accompany patients through picket lines, helping them avoid disgusting displays and name-calling. Some health facilities, like Clinica Eva in the Los Angeles suburb of El Monte, have relied on clinic defenders for several years.

Despite the ongoing violence against women's health clinics, the Federal Bureau of Investigation (FBI) has refused to become involved, claiming each is an isolated incident and not organized terrorism. Instead, the Bureau of Alcohol, Tobacco and Firearms is handling these cases. Only after a bomb destroyed a clinic near the White House in 1985 did Ronald Reagan utter a mild denunciation of the violence. States have, however, prosecuted under general criminal laws, or as in California and Massachusetts, they have passed special laws to deal with the problem.

Yet Joseph Scheidler's Pro-Action League continued, dubbing 1985 the "Year of Pain and Fear." They deliberately picketed hospitals, knowing that the only abortion provider in many parts of the United States is the local hospital. They also accelerated the number of direct actions.

To counter the violence and affirm women's right to abortion, the National Organization for Women (NOW) called a March for Women's Lives in March 1986 that coincided with International Women's Day. Approximately 125,000 women and men, representing all races, ages, nationalities, disabling conditions, and sexual orientations, marched past the White House to the Capitol in the largest pro-choice mobilization to date. Since that time, anti-abortion forces have been increasingly defensive.

The terror supported by some in the anti-abortion movement has also backfired even among its own ranks. The NRTL has publically criticized Scheidler. Cal Thomas of the Moral Majority has called the violence "deplorable." Some in the Catholic Church have denounced it as unprincipled and counterproductive. And splits remain in Congress over which type of legislation is best suited to make abortion illegal once more.

Efforts at Manipulation and Deception

The early 1980s saw new tactics in the anti-choice crusade. Moral Majority's Jerry Falwell declared 1982 the "Year of the Unborn Child" and called for donations to establish the "Save the Baby Ministry." Its purpose was to persuade women not to have abortions: "...little pregnant girls [sic] who have been put out of their homes by their parents can be placed in Christian homes where they are loved and ministered to on a daily basis." Fundamentalists claim to have set up hundreds of homes, providing for the needs of the woman and her baby up to one year—free, thanks to regular collections at fundamentalist churches.

Not content with Falwell's passive approach, Robert Pearson, a wealthy, Catholic real estate developer, devised a plan to set up "clinics" that would lure unsuspecting women. Once there, they are subjected to a barrage of anti-abortion propaganda. Pearson's film, "Education about Abortion," is calculated to deceive with emotional language and pictures of bloody full-term babies and women said to be suicidal after their abortions. His handbook includes everything from Biblical passages to read to incoming clients to fundraising techniques He suggests locating near an abortion clinic and using a name similar to that of a real provider. For example, the Fargo (North Dakota) Women's Health Organization had to deal with the Fargo Women's Help Organization.

Reproductive rights activists exposed, rallied, and petitioned against Pearson centers in California, New York, and Texas. Their efforts led to lawsuits brought by State Attorneys General charging consumer fraud, which forced the centers to close in some

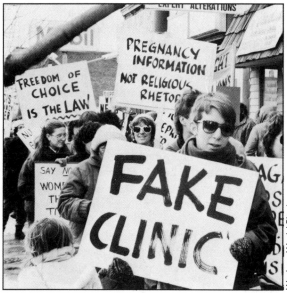

Workers World Photo

cases. In others, lawyers were able to force clinics to be upfront about listing themselves as abortion alternatives. Nonetheless, Pearson's tactics are still used in some states.

In 1985 the 28-minute film "Silent Scream" was given great publicity as the "Star Wars weapon for the pro-life movement." Narrated by Dr. Bernard Nathanson, a former pro-choice leader, the film records a sonogram of a 12-week-old fetus that Nathanson characterizes as moving away from a suction instrument and screaming in pain during an abortion. Medical evidence, however, proves this a fraud: A fetus moves reflexively and cannot feel pain until the 24th or 25th week. Nonetheless, this slick piece of propaganda was sent to every member of Congress and each Supreme Court Justice.

The overtly manipulative and hysterical tone of the film galvanized activists in the women's and progressive movements, who held forums, exposés, and teach-ins. As part of this response, Planned Parenthood made a pro-choice film called "Personal Decisions." In it, 6 women from different racial, religious, and class backgrounds explain their varied reasons for having abortions. For each, abortion provided a positive option in her life.

Other Anti-Abortion Efforts Defeated

Meanwhile, many opponents of abortion were still advocating legislation in Congress and the states. Early on, the centerpiece of their political agenda was the Family Protection Act (FPA), a New Right wish list. Although the FPA did not address abortion, it would have denied federal funds to school districts that used materials "tending to denigrate, diminish or deny the role differences between the sexes as they have traditionally been understood in the U.S."; to states that did not allow prayer in public schools; and to legal services agencies for litigation involving abortion, school desegregation, divorce, or gay rights. Supposedly promoting a "renaissance of the family," the bill was promoted at the same time that massive cuts in social service spending were destroying thousands of families by pushing them into poverty and out of their homes. Because of the vigilant struggle of many different civil rights groups, most of this repressive legislation was never passed.

In 1981, however, Congress passed a piece of the FPA: The Adolescent Family Life Act (the "Chastity Act") to discourage teen pregnancy and encourage adoption over abortion. Money was allocated to groups that gave religious instruction "to promote self-discipline and other prudent approaches to the problem of adolescent premarital sexual activity." Between 1982 when money was first appropriated and 1987 when such instruction was ruled unconstitutional by an appellate court, $92 million was spent on such programs. In July 1988 the Supreme Court reversed the lower court and ruled the act constitutional. Similarly, Reagan's Department of Health and Human Services (HHS) issued regulations, dubbed the "Squeal Rule," which forced federally funded family planning clinics to notify parents before prescribing contraceptives to unmarried minors. The courts found that there was no justification for these regulations and that they contradicted Congress's intent in establishing family planning programs.

Meanwhile, states continued to pass restrictions on abortion. In 1986 four states voted on referenda to curtail the use of local funds for Medicaid abortions. Thanks to the hard work of virtually every pro-choice group in the country, all four were defeated at the polls. In 1988, however, Arizona's legislature voted on a measure that would have banned abortion in that state. It was defeated by only one vote.

Pro-Choice Dissent within the Catholic Church

One of the most important signs of the fragmentation of the anti-abortion crusade is opposition within the Catholic Church itself. This development has been led by women. For instance, in 1982, after Sister Agnes Monsour was appointed head of the Michigan Department of Social Services, she was told to stop Medicaid funding for abortion, leave the job, or face a church trial. Although personally opposed to abortion, Monsour refused to impose her view on poor women and decided instead to leave her order.

In 1984, Vice-Presidential candidate Geraldine Ferraro, a pro-choice Catholic, prompted New York's Cardinal O'Connor to call abortion the crucial issue in the election and Ferraro a pariah. In response, a group of 24 nuns and 73 laypeople published a "Catholic Statement on Pluralism and Abortion" in the *New York Times*. It cited the diversity of opinion that exists on abortion among Roman Catholics and called for dialogue within the church. The Vatican ordered the nuns to recant. While many signed a retraction, two sisters refused. The charges against them were not dropped until June 1988.

Nonetheless, the public challenge prompted the church to crack down on dissent. Sarabeth Eason, an 11-year-old whose mother ran an abortion clinic, was forbidden to return to her Catholic school in Toledo, Ohio, because of her mother's public support for choice. She, in turn, criticized the school for including field trips to picket abortion facilities in its curriculum. Mary Ann Sorrentino, Director of Rhode Island Planned Parenthood, was excommunicated.

Catholic dissent continues to surface and opponents of church doctrine are visible and vocal. Groups like Catholics for a Free Choice are a constant thorn in the Vatican's side. In fact, the Catholic movement to stop abortion has proven ineffective within its own ranks. Approximately one-quarter of the 1.5 million women who abort each year are Roman Catholic, and 90 percent of Catholic women who are heterosexually active use a form of artificial contraception forbidden by the Church. Thirty-two percent say sexual activity between members of the same sex is not categorically wrong.

Continued Vigilance Required

The Reagan administration's latest tactic to bypass Congress and institute anti-abortion regulations has resulted in 1988 restrictions forbidding family planning clinics from including abortion in their counseling on pain of losing federal funding. The regulations are in abeyance due to challenges by state and local governments as well as the Reproductive Freedom Project of the American Civil Liberties Union.

Undaunted by ongoing legal and civil challenges, the administration has been most effective in taking its agenda overseas. During 1984-85 the International Planned Parenthood Federation (IPPF) lost $12 million--one-fourth of its budget—in federal funding because its programs in 12 of 100 countries includedabortion services. Similarly, the United Nations Family Planning Agency (UNFPA) had its allocation slashed by $10 million. Finally, the Agency for International Development (AID), ironically a major exporter of forced sterilization to the Third World during the 1960s and 1970s, is threatening to force the Planned Parenthood Federation of America (PPFA) to cease all abortion activities in exchange for its AID grant. PPFA is suing to stop them.

In spite of all these attacks, abortion remains legal and generally available in the United States, a daily reminder of the strength and promise of the women's movement. In this context, even the most extreme terror tactics must be viewed as a backhanded compliment. As the history of this backlash demonstrates, the right to abortion can only be preserved through constant vigilance and continuing commitment.

Chapter 8

Women's Lives: Recognizing Different Needs

Reproductive freedom encompasses a broad range of demands. While all women are discriminated against as women, the forms and effects of that discrimination depend on the particularity of individual women's lives. Such highly complex and varied factors as class, race, age, sexual preference, disabling condition, education, income, type of job, immigration status, religious/cultural background, and other social, economic, and cultural conditions all shape a woman's needs, options, and aspirations. Activists have not always understood the diversity of constraints restricting women's choices; this lack of understanding has impeded effort at organizing for reproductive freedom. Recognizing these differences is essential to our theory and practice.

Sexuality

Sexuality should be a strong source of individual pleasure and power. Women's delight in and control over their sexuality has been historically restricted, demeaned, and manipulated to suit men's needs, whether those of husband, slave master, homophobic society, or international population control agency. Women attaining positive feelings about their sexuality, with its many self-affirming relational, recreational, and reproductive possibilities, strikes at patriarchial social custom, as attested to by the recent backlash against feminism.

Society's view of women's sexuality is often contradictory. Young women are taught to hide their sexual interest and conform to the stereotype of sexual innocence, but their bodies and sexual attractiveness are routinely used to sell products, and sex is featured in most movies and TV shows. However, when women sell sexual services as prostitutes, they are treated as criminals. Pornography may also exploit and demean women's sexuality. Rape is a threat to all women, yet rape and other forms of sexual violence against women are still rampant and often go unpunished. Since the so-called sexual revolution in the early 1960s, many single women have become sexually active. Yet when they become pregnant, society offers little help. Although the stigma of adultery and illegitimacy has lessened somewhat, it is still used to punish women who are sexual outside of marriage.

Liberating women's sexuality requires knowledge about how our bodies function, sources of sexual pleasure either alone or with another, and the mechanics of conception, as well as access to safe, effective methods of limiting or promoting fertility. It is critical to overcome religious and social taboos against sex and sex education, particularly for teenage, single, or older women, lesbians, and women with disabling conditions. Although most people enjoy the role sex plays in their lives separate from reproduction, old attitudes remain. Sexuality is still only sanctioned in marriage, and homosexuality continues to be stigmatized. The 1987 Supreme Court upheld laws that make sodomy—any sexual activity other than the male-female missionary position—illegal.

This restrictive approach to sex contributes to the higher rate of teenage mothers in the United States than in other industrialized countries where young people have greater access to sex education, contraceptives, abortion, and social services. In 1982, almost half of all U.S. females aged 15-19 were sexually active. Of these slightly less than half used contraception, and 16 percent became pregnant. Of teenagers who become pregnant, 56 percent have babies.

The "pro-family" movement has responded to this trend with programs promoting "chastity," parental notification for abortion, and cutbacks in social services. However, a study by the National Academy of Sciences found no evidence that the availability of contraceptive services causes higher rates of sexual activity, unintended pregnancy, abortion, or births to unmarried teenagers. Data showed that after a school-based health clinic was set up in St. Paul, Minnesota, the student birthrate dropped from 79 to 26 per thousand.

Teens are not the only ones whose sexual needs are ignored. Studies at Duke University in the early 1970s show that 75 percent of women in their 70s feel sexual desire. As long as society views women's sexuality as tied to reproductive capacity, older women's sexual needs and activity remain invisible. Older women are seldom seen as appropriate or desirable sexual partners. Research is needed to determine the effects of pre- and postmenopausal hormonal cycles on older women's sexuality. A woman's need for full gynecological health care, including yearly pap tests and sexual counseling, continues throughout her life.

Lesbians are stigmatized, discriminated against, and physically assaulted because of their sexuality. Laws in many states criminalize homosexual acts. Often, lesbians do not have access to sex education or appropriate health care. There can be no real freedom of sexual choice and activity for anyone so long as homosexuality is proscribed.

There is also a tremendous bias against disabled women's sexual needs because it is presumed they are not sexually active and little or no provision is made for them to be sexual. Institutions are often strictly segregated by gender, so that residents have no opportunity for heterosexual activity. Severely disabled women in institutions run a high risk of being sexually abused by their caretakers and/or victims of sterilization abuse. Disabled women need special counseling about the possibilities for reproduction and about sexual and contraceptive techniques suited to their bodies.

Reproductive Health Services

Services for pregnancy, childbirth, abortion, sterilization, contraception, and reproductive technologies need to be equally available to all women. Many poor women—who include disproportionately high numbers of women of color because of institutionalized racism—receive inadequate or highly biased reproductive health care. One reason is that care is provided on a fee-for-service basis, rather than need. In 1986 less than 0.003 percent of the federal budget was devoted to reproductive health, including research and subsidies for poor women.

• *Pregnancy and Childbirth*

If a woman does not have either her own or a partner's medical insurance to cover a private gynecologist, she must find a public clinic in a hospital to care for her during pregnancy and childbirth. Because the 1980s saw cutbacks in such services, many poor women lack proper prenatal medical care. Cutbacks in the Women, Infants and Children (WIC) Program have also reduced pre- and postnatal nutritional food supplements to poor women. Many factors, all related to poverty, yield rising infant mortality rates in Black, Latin, Asian, and Native American communities, comparable to or higher than those in Third World countries.

Women with disabilities, lesbians, and single women often en-
counter problems when they want to get pregnant. Physicians often
discourage women with disabilities from having children because of
the special care they require during pregnancy and childbirth. Lesbians
who want to be mothers may be deprived of fertility planning services
and the new technologies (see Chapter 4). Lesbians may not use contraceptives, but they do require yearly medical exams, pap tests, and
supportive, understanding gynecological care.

• Abortion

Abortion may be legal, but it is not equally accessible to all
women. Women in rural areas may have to travel hundreds of miles
for abortion services, and some health insurance plans, notably those
of federal employees, do not include coverage for abortion. Parental

notification and consent requirements in 20 states present major hurdles
for young women seeking abortions (see Chapter 5), who may suffer
health risks when abortions are delayed. For many poor women, often
young and women of color, the average 1986 cost of $213 for an abor-
tion presents a formidable obstacle.

Poor women on Medicaid have not received federal funding for
abortion except under extremely limited circumstances since 1980

when the Hyde Amendment resulted in the reduction of annual reimbursed procedures from about 300,000 to 3,000. Women in 14 states and the District of Columbia still have state funding, but women in other states must sacrifice their families' survival needs in order to pay for abortions. For example, the average family of 4 relying on Aid to Families with Dependent Children in Missouri receives $250 a month, while the average cost of abortion in that state is $150. The Alan Guttmacher Institute estimates that 20 percent of poor women carry unwanted pregnancies to term because they cannot afford abortion services.

Even poor women living in states that do subsidize abortions do not have guaranteed access. Only 39 percent of nonhospital facilities (usually less costly than hospitals) accept state Medicaid reimbursements, and only 55 percent offer reduced fees to poor patients.

The threat of abortion abuse also exists. Women infected with the AIDS virus may be pressured to abort, although only 30-50 percent of fetuses percent become infected. Women of color may feel enormous pressure due to oppressive social conditions. It should be noted that in New York City before 1970, Black and Puerto Rican women accounted for 80 percent of the deaths due to illegal abortion. Currently, women of color are between 2 and 3 times as likely to obtain abortions as are white women. The distinction must be made between choosing an abortion and needing one to avert the effects of a racist society.

• *Sterilization*

All women and men who wish to permanently end their reproductive capacity should be able to obtain needed services. However, as discussed in Chapter 3, government sterilization funding policies have resulted in a bias against poor women, women with disabling conditions, and women of color that promotes population control rather than reproductive freedom.

Although federal regulations were passed in 1979 to stop sterilization abuse, it still occurs due to oppressive social conditions, among other factors. Women infected with the AIDS virus may be coerced into becoming sterilized. Women workers' rights are jeopardized when they are asked to become sterilized in order keep a job or they are excluded from jobs simply because of their childbearing potential. In 1977 women workers at American Cyanamid were forced to undergo sterilization in order to keep their jobs. The Lead Industries Association has publicly opposed the employment of fertile women since 1974. Studies show, however, equal risk to men's fertility. The solution lies

National Lesbian and Gay March on Washington, D.C., 1987.

not in tampering with women's bodies, but in improving working conditions for both women and men.

Social Conditions for Parenting

A wide variety of conditions must be met to help people be parents. The decision not to have children is all too often based on the lack of adequate childcare, education, housing, and jobs.

• *Medical Care*

All women need medical care in order to be healthy and give birth to healthy babies. Yet only 3 percent of the federal budget is allotted for health care, in contrast to over 50 percent for defense and related military services. Because the health care system is based on payment for services, instead of on need, many women are not able to provide basic health care for themselves or their children.

The current system of private medical insurance is grossly inadequate. Part-time, minimum-wage, or nonunion jobs that many women must take often do not provide insurance. Lesbians and unmarried women are rarely eligible for their partners' coverage. Unemployed people rarely have insurance. In fact, 37 million people in the United

States in 1988 have no medical insurance at all. Although Medicaid and Medicare were set up in the 1960s to cover medical costs for the poor and elderly, many women fall through the cracks in these inefficient, bureaucratic systems, which were themselves seriously cut back during the 1980s.

Racism plays a devastating role in denying people needed health care. In the last decade high double-digit unemployment among Black, Latin, and Native American communities, coupled with cutbacks in nutrition and health care programs, has led to a sharp rise in diseases related to hunger and poverty such as rickets and tuberculosis. Since medical services have never been adequately provided in domestic Third World communities, the nationwide trend toward privatization and closing of city hospitals limits care even more. The AIDS crisis, which is reaching epidemic proportions in some Black and Latin communities, has become a serious drain on medical facilities that are already strained to the breaking point.

• *Childcare*

The need for childcare outside the home emerged as a major social problem in the 1970s as women joined the paid workforce in huge numbers, but there has been no national response to this need. The United States is the only industrialized nation that does not provide paid parental leaves after childbirth and childcare for infants and school-age children. Only 40 percent of women receive leaves of any kind. Disability benefits may be available in certain circumstances pre- and post-childbirth. The vast majority of women must seek individual childcare solutions, often at great expense.

More affluent women can afford to hire other women (often young, immigrant, or women of color, who have historically been exploited as childcare workers) to care for their children. The vast majority of working and poor women, however, are limited by what they can afford and by what services are available in their neighborhoods. Childcare costs can be deducted from income taxes, but allowances are minimal. Only a tiny minority of businesses provide on-site childcare or childcare allotments in employee benefits, have flexible hours, and grant time off so workers can tend sick children.

Both parent and child need a time of adjustment after birth. Parents would be more efficient on the job if they knew their children were adequately taken care of. Divorced and single mothers would not have to rely on welfare if they could find affordable, quality childcare and work at livable wages. A national program of comprehensive childcare is long overdue, with the long-term perspective of freeing women from obligatory primary responsibility for childrearing.

• *Education*

Although, in theory, universal education exists for all children beginning at the age of 5, in practice there is tremendous disparity in the *quality* of education in the United States. Racial segregation, class inequities (allotments for education frequently depend on the tax base of the local school district), and discrimination against children with disabling conditions are primary factors in limiting educational opportunities in poor, Black, Latin, Asian, and Native American communities and rural areas. Rising dropout rates from high school and increasing illiteracy are two serious problems that limit people's options as parents and workers.

Special early childhood programs like Head Start were initiated during the 1960s to counter the legacy of racism and encourage children of color to excel in school. Studies have shown their effectiveness, as high numbers of students graduate from high school and go on to college. Instead of being expanded in the 1980s, however, they have been cut, like other needed educational services. The enrollment of people of color in colleges and universities dropped significantly in the 1980s as funding for higher education was also cut.

Special programs have been set up for "displaced homemakers" —women who need to earn a living after working many years in the home. Often divorced or widowed, these women are taught skills to help them get jobs and function on their own. Some communities also have programs to teach young mothers parenting skills, so that women who were abused or neglected as children can learn how to care for children and end generational cycles of misery and despair. Unfortunately, these programs are rarely available.

• *Housing*

Women and children are joining the ranks of the homeless in huge numbers because of a housing crisis for poor and working people, especially in Third World communities. The lack of federally funded housing for the poor and the gentrification of poor neighborhoods has resulted in a shortage of affordable housing. Women with disabling conditions and older women have special housing needs that are also going unmet.

- ### Jobs and Pay Equity

What people can provide for their families is determined by their ability to pay. Financially, women's choices are severely limited due to segregation in lower-paying jobs (see Chapter 6). Access to the full range of jobs, pay equity, and ending sexual harassment and bias against women with children would go a long way toward ending discrimination against women workers. Raising the minimum wage and strengthening unions are concrete ways of increasing women's ability to care for their families, whether they are women of color, teenagers, older, single, divorced, lesbian, disabled, or undocumented.

Fighting Back

This brief survey of the many factors affecting women's lives reveals why historically it has been so difficult to organize a unified movement for reproductive freedom. Different organizational approaches stem from different life views and experiences. For example, some white, middle-class women have seen the movement for legal abortion as a single-issue struggle. In contrast, women of color view the struggle for women's health care within the overall campaign to end racist inequities throughout society. But there are differences even within these groups. Some white women support abortion rights as part of a strategy for population control, while some Black women oppose abortion precisely because it has been used as a genocidal tool.

When women have organized for reproductive freedom, the failure to recognize and deal with these differences has sometimes led to painful and immobilizing splits. The inability to build an ongoing mass movement is in part due to differences that have separated, rather than enriched us. Women are often so mired in the problems of daily survival that reproductive issues seem irrelevant except when particular needs arise. Adults find it hard to reach out to teenagers in constructive ways. Straight women may not understand gay women's problems or sympathize with their needs. Able-bodied women may forget to consider the needs of women with disabling conditions. Racism and its many subtleties raise barriers to joint organizing. Class also divides women where better educated, highly skilled women tend to dominate in leadership roles. Identifying commonalities and building upon them are necessary to creating and sustaining a truly multiracial, multiclass movement for reproductive freedom that both recognizes and honors the particularities and needs of all women.

Chapter 9

Organizing for Reproductive Freedom

Challenges to reproductive freedom continue to arise, with legal abortion the frequent target. In recently initiated law suits men sued to prevent abortions of fetuses they claim to have fathered and asserted their right to monetary damages if abortions were performed. In May 1988, "Operation Rescue," a militant organization of anti-abortionists led by Randall Terry and Joseph Scheidler, garnered police cooperation and broad media attention when it staged sit-ins closing several small abortion clinics in New York. Although pro-choice groups mounted an impressive counteroffensive, the foes of abortion were nevertheless emboldened and have gone on to attempt to shut down clinics in other cities. With Reagan appointees filling 47 percent of all federal judicial seats in this country and with the current anti-choice majority on the Supreme Court, increasingly successful legal challenges to *Roe v. Wade* are sure to arise in the coming years. Indeed, a Reagan-dominated U.S. Circuit Court of Appeals in August 1988 upheld a two-parent notification statute for unmarried teenagers despite clear evidence that it imposed enormous burdens on them.

Such attacks make it critical to continue organizing for reproductive freedom. While some single-issue abortion groups use the language of reproductive freedom, it is highly unlikely they will promote a reproductive freedom agenda. Our current view, based on our experience in CARASA, is that while we must continue to build reproductive freedom organizations, this agenda should be integrated into all political programs as a *paradigm* of what it means to have autonomy and power.

Most people think of reproductive freedom only when they hear about specific issues of abortion or sterilization abuse. Our movement must show how reproductive freedom is an essential component in every struggle for social justice. Activists must understand that reproductive freedom promotes everyone's interests—men's as well as women's—as it challenges the very social, economic, and political roots of the system under which we live. As activists recognized over a century ago, without advances in reproductive freedom, women's participation in broader social struggles is hampered. In the final analysis, women's oppression in a sexist, racist, homophobic society can only end when there is reproductive freedom.

The movement for reproductive freedom grew largely out of the women's liberation movement, but we cannot take our connection to the current women's movement for granted. We must reaffirm and insist on the centrality of reproductive freedom in all feminist struggle.

Women are already in the forefront of many struggles for social justice, such as those against nuclear war and for decent housing, pay equity, welfare, and social services. Realistically, these issues loom larger in people's day-to-day lives than general needs for abortion or freedom from sterilization abuse. However, these issues can be seen as components of reproductive freedom and work on them will benefit from the incorporation of a reproductive freedom perspective.

Our formulation of reproductive freedom allows us to share common ground with many progressive movements. In the union movement, for example, such issues as childcare, benefits for partners of lesbians, gay men, and unmarried people, and medical care that includes abortion coverage are being raised on the job and written into contracts. The disability rights movement is asserting disabled people's rights to be sexual and have families. In addition to general opposition to racism, we support efforts of the anti-racist struggle to end high infant mortality, deal positively with teenage pregnancy, and educate people about all forms of fertility control. Showing solidarity with international struggles, whether in South Africa or Central America, includes exposing the role of the United States in dumping experimental forms of fertility control and exporting sterilization abuse to the Third World. We share the aims of the peace and ecology movements to make the world a safe and healthy place for all children and of the gay and lesbian movement to reconstruct the "family." Other movements may arise with which our agenda has an obvious affinity, for example, organizing for a comprehensive national health care system that is not based on profit and promotes prevention of illness.

Over the last 10 years, we have been heartened as issues of reproductive freedom have been incorporated in various coalition struggles. They were among many demands in the anti-war march

Joyce Chediac/Workers World Photo

Reproductive Freedom Week, New York, 1988.

against the Pentagon on May 3, 1981, and then in 1983 on the 20th anniversary of the civil rights march on Washington. The 1987 Lesbian and Gay March on Washington was truly exemplary: Reproductive freedom was included as one of eight overall demands. Continuing to build and work in multi-issue coalitions is required so that the struggle for reproductive freedom is included in many kinds of educational and organizing work.

We see a long-term struggle that requires a radical social, economic, and political transformation of society. It is essential that reproductive freedom be incorporated in that vision. We know that establishing social justice is only the first step toward ending all forms of discrimination and oppression and truly empowering all women.

Below are a few of the many relevant books that illuminate the issues discussed in this pamphlet. Space does not permit us to include any of the excellent articles, periodicals and pamphlets on these topics.

Barbara Bergmann, *The Economic Emergence of Women* (New York: Basic Books, 1988).

The Boston Women's Health Book Collective, *The New Our Bodies Ourselves: A Book By and For Women* (New York: Simon & Schuster, 1984).

Charlotte Bunch, *Passionate Politics: Essays 1968-1986* (New York: St. Martin's Press, 1988).

Allen Chase, *The Legacy of Malthus* (New York: Knopf, 1977).

Wendy Chavkin (ed.), *Double Exposure: Women's Health Hazards on the Job and at Home* (New York: Monthly Review Press, 1984).

Johnetta B. Cole (ed.), *All American Women: Lines That Divide, Ties That Bind* (New York: The Free Press/MacMillan Inc., 1986).

Gena Corea, *The Mother Machine* (New York: Harper & Row, 1986).

Paula Brown Doress and others in cooperation with the Boston Women's Health Book Collective, *Ourselves Growing Older: Women Aging with Knowledge and Power* (New York: Simon & Schuster, 1987).

Michelle Fine and Adrienne Asch (eds.), *Women with Disabilities: Essays in Psychology, Culture and Politics* (Philadelphia: Temple University Press, 1988).

Jay L. Garfield and Patricia Hennessy (eds.), *Abortion: Moral and Legal Perspectives* (Amherst: University of Massachusetts Press, 1984)

Linda Gordon, *Woman's Body, Woman's Right: A Social History of Abortion in America* (New York: Penguin Books, 1977, revised 1989).

Beverly Wildung Harrison, *Our Right to Choose: Towards a New Ethic of Abortion* (Boston: Beacon Press, 1983).

Betsy Hartmann, *Reproductive Rights and Wrongs: The Global Politics of Population Control and Contraceptive Choice* (New York: Harper & Row Perennial Library, 1987).

Bell Hooks, *Feminist Theory: From Margin to Center* (Boston: South End Press, 1984).

Gloria I. Joseph and Jill Lewis, *Common Differences: The Conflicts in Black and White Feminist Perspectives* (Boston: South End Press, 1981).

Judith Lasker and Susan Borg, *In Search of Parenthood: Coping with Infertility and High-Tech Conception* (Boston: Beacon Press, 1988).

Lesbian Psychologies Collective, *Lesbian Psychologies: Explorations and Challenges* (Urbana: University of Illinois Press, 1987).

Kristin Luker, *Abortion and the Politics of Motherhood* (Berkeley: University of California Press, 1985).

Kathleen McDonnell, *Not An Easy Choice: A Feminist Re-Examines Abortion* (Boston: South End Press, 1984).

James C. Mohr, *Abortion in America: The Origins and Evolution of National Policy* (New York: Oxford University Press, 1978).

Rosalind Pollack Petchesky, *Abortion and Woman's Choice: The State, Sexuality and Reproductive Freedom* (Boston: Northeastern University Press, 1985).

Thomas M. Shapiro, *Population Control Politics: Women, Sterilization and Reproductive Choice* (Philadelphia: Temple University Press, 1985).

Ann Snitow, Christine Stansell, and Sharon Thompson (eds.), *Powers of Desire: The Politics of Sexuality* (New York: Monthly Review Press, 1983).

Kristin Stallard, Barbara Ehrenreich and Holly Sklar, *Poverty in the American Dream: Women and Children First* (Boston: South End Press, 1983).

Michelle Stanworth (ed.), *Reproductive Technologies: Gender, Motherhood and Medicine* (Minneapolis: University of Minnesota Press, 1987).

Catherine R. Stimpson and Ethel Spector Person (eds.), *Women, Sex and Sexuality* (Chicago: University of Chicago Press, 1980).